To Maru Skeen,
Whose gold El Camino
is being driven in this
series.

John Hanson
February, 2018

THE NEW DARKNESS

The End of Ozzie and Harriet

Second Edition

"The world will not be destroyed by those who do evil, but by those who watch them without doing anything."

Albert Einstein

John Hansen

BOOK TWO of
THE BLUESUIT CHRONICLES
Based on Actual Events

The Bluesuit Chronicles: The New Darkness – Second Edition

ISBN: 1548825832
ISBN: 13: 9781548825836

Published and Printed by
CreateSpace

Cover design by Ira Mandas and Tonsmeire Studios
Printed in the United States of America

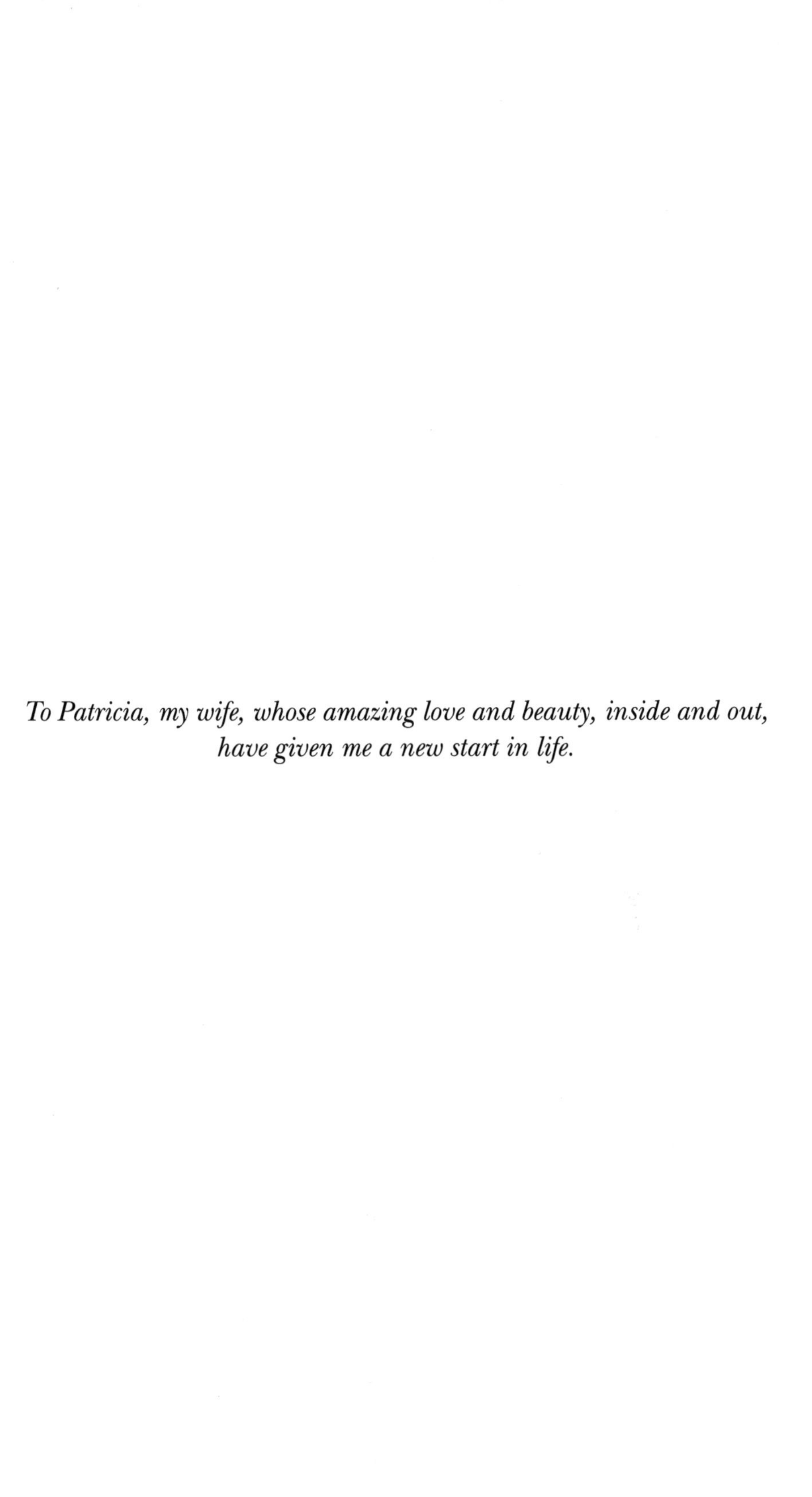

To Patricia, my wife, whose amazing love and beauty, inside and out, have given me a new start in life.

DEDICATION

This book is dedicated to the law enforcement officers of America---past, present and future--and to the unseen personnel who support their work: the photographers, dispatchers, records clerks, evidence custodians, crime lab technicians, fingerprint experts, legal advisors and the administrators too, for without them protecting the public would not be possible.

"Bluesuits" was the traditional FBI term during the 60s and 70s for non-federal, law enforcement officers; city, county or state agencies. The Bluesuit Chronicles series is historical fiction dedicated to telling the untold story of suburban and rural law enforcement officers during the explosive, transitional 1970s decade. Returning Vietnam veterans were scorned as "baby killers" by their peers who stayed home and taunted police officers as "pigs." Decades later, in the 21st Century, their legacy of holding the line against anarchy and willingness to sacrifice for the greater good, is carried on by the quiet warrior-heroes of today -- our police.

THE BACKSTORY

Riots, demonstrations, rampant crime and distrust of government had already arrived on the American scene during the 60s. Strong leadership and a sense of direction were lacking during. Social collapse was spreading. It became every man for himself, and the mission to stop the spread of communism in Vietnam became a quagmire.

The new darkness that settled over America wasn't a failed presidency, or the emergence of home-grown terrorist groups. It was the drug epidemic that tore families apart, and either ruined or ended the lives of thousands in the Baby Boom generation.

The patriotic fervor of President John F. Kennedy was replaced as if it had never happened by a self-destructive zeal for getting high on marijuana, LSD, cocaine and heroin. The drug craze swept through the great American middle class like fire. Mainline churches were dead; marriage and family were renounced as shackles. The new values of "free love" and "do your own thing" led to a rising divorce rate, unwanted children, unwed mothers, dysfunctional families and new strains of venereal disease.

Standing in the gap in that time of unprecedented evil were society's protectors, the sheep dogs, the "Bluesuits."

ACKNOWLEDGEMENTS

Special thanks to my beautiful, loving wife Patricia for her support, patience and help with beta reading; to my longtime friend and high school classmate, artist Ira Mandas, for another excellent cover design and to Tonsmeire Studios for cover and title lettering for the revised cover. This would not be a series if not for Larry Siferd, who suggested the writing of actual police experiences as a series. The medical science background off my friend Will Marriott made possible the details of drug abuse and addiction for this book. I am also grateful to Tina Williams for editing and proof reading. This series would be possible without the help of various retired members of the Bellevue and Seattle Police Departments who coached me on placing major events in chronological order.

A REVIEW FROM AMAZON.COM

"Book Two of The Bluesuit Chronicles series, *The New Darkness,* continues the story of Vietnam veteran Roger Hitchcock, now a police officer in Bellevue, Washington. The spreading new drug culture is exacting a heavy toll on Hitchcock's generation. Some die, some are permanently impaired, everyone is impacted by this wave of evil that even turns traditional values inside out. Like other officers, the times test Hitchcock: will he resign in disgust, become hardened and bitter, corrupt, or will his background in competition boxing and military combat experience enable him to rise to meet the challenge? Romance, intrigue, and action are the fabric of *The New Darkness.*"

A READER COMMENTS ON THE COVER OF *THE NEW DARKNESS*

"John — On the cover of *The New Darkness*, Hitchcock's expression conveys the mood of the title, and conveys to me (*without reading the text*) that the Rookie is at that point where he recognizes and accepts the hard reality of the job and times that you so well presented in the previous foreword. It is likely a point where many break, or become bitter or disillusioned.

Some, I imagine, quit, radically change their character or personality, become callous, or possibly corrupt. Others rise to the challenge and grow into effective Officers, never compromising their principles, though personally taking a lot of hits.

Looking forward to the read,

John Schweisow
Scottsdale, Arizona

READER REVIEWS

"As expected, Hansen doesn't disappoint his readers. The action starts right away, holding attention with the interesting characters all through the book. His resolution of many unexpected situations leaves us wanting more."

N. Meyn, Redmond, WA

"Great book that really gets into the minds of officers who went through the growing pains of that era. As a police officer who worked briefly with John during that era, it brought back a lot of memories of serving during that time. It is pretty darn accurate." Jim Hassinger, Bellevue, WA

"As a former Bellevue police officer who worked for many years with John Hansen, I know him and his style. In this series of books, he presents an easy to read, yet suspenseful and well-crafted narrative. His ability to tell a story, often based on the reality of policing, is excellent, and the way he leaves the reader in a cliff-hanger sort of way at the end of each book in the series certainly drives the reader to want to follow the story. John is a great writer and has done well in the series. I strongly urge him to continue writing. As he does I will be his first customer. Well done, John. "

P. Cooper, Mukilteo, WA

"John Hansen is getting very good at developing his story-line and his characters. This book is a great way to spend the time waiting for a ferry or airplane and having the time go by in a hurry, I am very much awaiting the third book in the series and although one book does lead you into the next - each book stands on its own as a good yarn of the police work of the 1970's. The only reason I did not rate this with a 5th Star is because I didn't want it to end.......... "

Milo Walker, Port Angeles, WA

"Wow!" By E.M. Hammond, Arizona author

"This is a great read! Best so far in the series...has good insight from a police officer's point of view during dangerous and trying situations--shows both professional and personal emotions---looking forward to the next book..."

Aubrey Aramaki, Issaquah, WA

PREFACE

Don't expect closure or tidy endings to the situations in this series. The books in *The Bluesuit Chronicles* are not traditional novels that follow a plot from beginning to conclusion, as in the rebellion-ruin-restoration formula. Real life doesn't follow a script, and this series is about real life, history portrayed through fictional characters. The setting is a small town that became a big town almost overnight. Its inexperienced police department grows and matures as it encounters unprecedented cultural, political, and violent opposition on every level while struggling to meet the demands of our most troubling times since the Civil War.

Police officers and detectives can't and don't solve every crime. Criminals sometimes evade justice on the basis of a legal technicality, a smart defense attorney, or a weak prosecutor, judge or jury. The cops might get another shot at bringing them to justice, but usually it doesn't happen. Real life is unscripted. Cops become cynical. They face unending conflict on the streets, within their own departments, within city hall. Not every issue is resolved; not every betrayer and hidden agenda is found out.

CHAPTER 1

A LITTLE MOONLIGHT MADNESS

Under a full moon so brilliant it rivaled a cloudy afternoon, Hitchcock arrived at the street where the domestic violence (DV) call was. Sherman tapped his cruiser brake-lights briefly to signal his location across the street and one house away from the scene. He cut his headlights and parked behind Sherman.

The scene of the call was a split-level home with dark wood siding. Lights were on inside and drapes were drawn across the huge second--floor picture windows. Without exchanging greetings Hitchcock and Sherman stood beside their patrol cars in silence, listening for noises inside the house. It was too quiet for a family beef.

"I've been here before," Sherman said in a low voice. "They're Hungarian immigrants. Parents, two teenage kids. The old man is a boozer, big, very strong, loves to fight. The full moon stirs him up every month."

"What happened last time?"

"His wife and teenage son both needed stitches. Otis and I fought him every step of the way from here to the booking room."

"Anything happen while I was on my way?"

"I heard the wife crying inside when I first got here, but it stopped," Sherman said.

"Let's hope she didn't stop because she's dead. I hate DV calls."

"Yeah!" Sherman said with a grin. He liked working with Hitchcock.

They paused at the front door to listen. A television overrode the sounds of arguing voices—a woman either crying or begging and a man's voice that sounded threatening. The words were unintelligible.

They stood on either side of the door as Sherman knocked. No answer. He tried the doorbell----it didn't work. Sherman pounded louder this time.

"Police officers! Open the door!"

No response. Sherman tried the door. It opened. The lighting was dim. The noise of the television and the indistinct sobbing of a woman filled the air as they crossed the threshold.

Hitchcock didn't like any of it.

"Police officers! We're coming in!" Sherman loudly announced.

A disheveled, middle-aged woman with defeat etched into the lines of her face, came from the hallway to the top of the stairs. She was distraught and crying, and covered with one hand her bleeding mouth; her left eye was black and almost swollen shut. Sherman and Hitchcock went up the stairs. Hitchcock gently checked her face, noting defense wounds on her forearms.

"What happened, Katalin?" Sherman asked. "Who did this to you? Was it---"

"Yaus. Lajos, who ulse?" she sobbed in her thick Eastern European accent.

"Where is he now? Where are the children?"

"Children hiding downstairs again, afraid! Lajos is in da' den, down hall, dat way," she said, indicating the location of the den with a nod.

Hitchcock checked her pupils with his flashlight. They were uneven. "You have a head concussion, Ma'am. Let's get you and your kids out of the house and to the hospital. I'll call an ambulance."

Sherman escorted Katalin and her children outside while Hitchcock guarded the hallway in case Lajos attacked. Before he returned to the house, Sherman radioed for an ambulance. He and Hitchcock placed the family in Sherman's patrol car and stayed with them until the hearse from Flintoft's Mortuary of Issaquah that did double-duty as an ambulance service for the City, arrived.

They knew Lajos was in the house, alone, drinking. The waiting was tense.

Suddenly a long, deep primal scream erupted from within the house. It stopped everyone outside. Hitchcock wouldn't have been surprised to hear a gun go off in the house next.

"Are there any guns in the house?" Hitchcock asked Katalin as he cleaned and applied a gauze bandage to her eye, now swollen shut.

"No, guns," she said.

"Any knives or other weapons?"

She shook her head.

"You're sure he has no weapons?" Hitchcock asked again.

Katalin blinked her one good eye at Sherman and Hitchcock as she held her hand over her bleeding mouth.

"Lajos, he need no knife or weapon. He kuhl men before, with bare hand. He wait for you now, he know I call you, he want to fight you, he say he will beat *you* this time, maybe kuhl you," she mumbled meekly.

Two men in a Flintoft's hearse arrived. They began checking the children and the mother after Sherman briefed them.

Sherman took Hitchcock aside. "Lajos played possum when Otis and I were called here last month," he said in a hushed voice.

"Possum?"

"He ignored us at first and then acted friendly so we thought he would go with us peaceably. When our guard was down, he attacked. If Otis hadn't been with me I would have wound up in the hospital."

"What's the plan?"

"Little talk----if he balks at obeying us, we take him on."

"Sounds like a plan, Stan. Let's go," Hitchcock said with a confident grin.

Lajos Csizmadia sat in his busted down brown vinyl recliner with his feet up, staring at the television. He didn't look up or turn around when Hitchcock and Sherman approached him from behind.

He was powerfully built in the manner of an ape. The muscles of his long arms were like the huge ropes that tie sea-going ships to piers. His hands were huge and meaty. He stank of beer, cigarettes and stale sweat. His khaki pants were filthy, and his hairy pot-belly bulged out from under his grimy white t-shirt. A half-empty pack of Pall Malls cigarettes, a Zippo lighter and an overflowing ashtray were on the side table next to him.

To impress the officers, Csizmadia picked up a fresh Olympia beer bottle from the floor and flipped the cap off with just a flick of his thumb. Hitchcock and Sherman looked at each other. A few more seconds of silence passed. The scuff marks on Lajos' knuckles did not escape Hitchcock's notice.

"Lajos, your wife has head injuries. She says you hit her. We want to hear your side of it," Sherman finally said.

"Yeh, she's always bitchin' 'bout somethin'. You know how it is wi' wimmen. No udder way to shut 'er up," he said with a shrug of his shoulders and a grin. He took another swig of his beer and smiled as he let out a long belch that fouled the air.

Lajos glanced up at Hitchcock, who stood over him, glaring. "Wot th' hell do you thenk you are doing, staring at me like dat, eh?"

"Just wondering what kind of man hits a woman. No real *man* does that, only low-down cowards like *you* beat women," Hitchcock said in a jeering tone.

Lajos turned in his chair, looked Hitchcock up and down and turned away as he snorted, "So wat, eh?"

Sherman rolled his eyes and shook his head when Hitchcock leaned over and whispered in a mocking tone in Csizmadia's ear, "You like to beat children too, I bet. Only COWARDS do that!" Hitchcock, said, shouting the word coward.

An evil grin darkened Csizmadia's face as if this was the moment he was waiting for. "Yah? Let me remind you—this is *my* house you are in, Officer! You get out of my house or I throw you both out!" he bellowed, setting his beer on the side table and his feet on the floor.

Hoping to avoid another brawl, Sherman tried to calm the situation. "Sure, Lajos, we're leaving. I am sorry but you have to go with us. You're under arrest for assault. You have the right to remain silent. Anything you say will---"

Sherman never finished the Miranda warnings. The second he touched Lajos's left arm, the fight was on.

"Nem! Ez alkalommal fogom verni titeket!" Csizmadia shouted (Hungarian for "No! This time I will beat you both!") Growling like a bear, he leaped out of his recliner in a fury and attacked Sherman and Hitchcock at once, throwing punches wildly.

Hitchcock and Sherman rushed him on either side, crashing over the wood coffee table and television console, as they wrestled him to the floor, finally pinning his arms to his sides. He continued fighting with his feet, kicking viciously and twisting his trunk in a struggle to break free. Csizmadia was even stronger than he appeared. He began a series of loud bellowing sounds that sounded like a mature bull. "AHHH! AHHH! AHHH!" Each blast from his lungs stank worse than his body odor and seemed to increase his strength.

Where's Walker when we need him? Hitchcock thought briefly. Holding Csizmadia's left arm against his body, Sherman motioned to Hitchcock with his eyes. Together they rolled him toward Hitchcock to get him onto his stomach.

Csizmadia growled and resisted mightily like a cornered bull. He craned his neck, rapidly snapping his teeth like a dog in an effort to bite Hitchcock's arm as he was being rolled over. Hitchcock moved his arm out of the way just in time. He placed his right knee between Csizmadia's shoulder blades, pressing every ounce of his hundred-ninety-five pounds into his upper back while Sherman pulled his wrists together and snapped the cuffs on.

Straining for breath under Hitchcock's weight, his face squished into the carpet, Csizmadia relaxed, and smiled. "Okay, boys, yeh, I give up, I give up. I fight no more. You boys win again," he said between gasps.

They stood him up. "Lajos," Sherman said, "the law says we have to take you to jail. Will you go with us without any more trouble?"

Csizmadia's face was red, the veins of his bull neck bulged like blue hoses under his skin, black greasy hair covered his eyes, his bad breath polluted the air from panting heavily. His smile was an evil smile as he nodded and panted, trying to catch his breath.

Sherman caught Hitchcock's attention and shook his head as a way of saying silently *"ain't no way is this guy done."*

Hitchcock nodded that he understood. He placed his right hand on Csizmadia's right arm and his left hand on the top of his shoulder at the base of the neck as a way of knowing when he was about to spring into another attack.

In an instant he felt Csizmadia's shoulders tense when they reached the door. He suddenly spun around, bent over and charged Hitchcock, throwing his body-weight into him to crush him against the door frame.

Hitchcock was knocked backward but deftly slipped aside just in time so that Csizmadia's main energy caused him to slam himself head-first into the door frame. He shook his head, turned and charged Hitchcock again, head down like a bull. Twisting, kicking and head-butting while straining against the handcuffs, he roared like an animal "ARRRRRGH!" UUUUUGHAH!"

Csizmadia dropped to the floor. His feet flashed out at Hitchcock and Sherman in vicious kicks He tried to head-butt them when they stood him up. Holes in the sheetrock walls were created during the struggle.

Sherman slipped his baton between the handcuffs, placed the tip on the middle of Csizmadia's back, and lifted up. The excruciating pain penetrated his fog of rage and alcohol, forcing him to bend forward from the waist.

The three men staggered together down the hall, down the stairs to the front door. They half-dragged, half-carried him outside, kicking and spitting everywhere. Then he saw his terrified family.

"I weel keel you all, your wives and children too for taking my family! Yeh! You wait 'til I get out jail—I find you! I burn your houses down! I keel your dogs and cats!" Lajos bellowed, his mouth spraying saliva at the cowering team from Flintoff's who were treating his family for injuries.

Neighbors stood speechless on their front doorsteps, watching. Csizmadia cried out to them. "Help me! The police they are taking me to kill me! Stop them, please" he shouted all the way down the street to Sherman's cruiser.

Hitchcock opened the door, bent Csizmadia over and shoved him in, head-first.

"Why are you putting him in my car?" Sherman asked.

"Your district, your boy."

"Thanks, Roger!"

Hitchcock smiled.

Sherman's ears were ringing by the time he reached the station, where Hitchcock waited for him. They were kicked and bitten several times each as they wrestled Csizmadia out of the patrol car, nearly breaking the station door as they fought their way through it. A terrified Lieutenant Bostwick, shaking in his shoes, wide-eyed, hid in an alcove by the coffee machine as the prisoner fought the officers every inch of the hallway, grunting and snorting like an enraged bull, kicking and throwing himself into Hitchcock, then Sherman, until at last they wrestled him into an empty holding cell and removed the handcuffs. They were both out of breath as they returned to their patrol cars.

Dispatch had another call waiting when they called in: "Both units check the status of Three Zero Eight and Three Zero Seven at a fight involving twenty or more minors at the dance at Lake Hills Roller Rink, NE 8th and 164th Avenue. Neither unit has come back on the air in over ten minutes, and no one is answering the phone at the rink. Code Two."

Hitchcock flipped his overhead light on and sped the three-mile straightaway of NE 8th to the call, with Sherman following. A crowd of over twenty teenagers was milling around the dirt parking lot when they arrived. Neither Walker nor Otis were to be seen. Hitchcock keyed his radio mike:

> "Both units have arrived at Lake Hills Dance. Got a large crowd of juvies in the parking lot. Patrol cars are here, no officers visible. I'll be out of the car."
>
> "I'd better stay with our vehicles," Sherman said.

The crowd of teenagers began spouting the standard insults.

"Hey look, more pigs are here!"

"Oink! Oink!"

"I smell bacon!"

Two males were sitting on the hood of a black-and-white patrol car. "Get off the patrol car, right now," Hitchcock said.

"Up yours, pig," the bigger of the two replied.

Hitchcock pushed him off the patrol car so hard he landed butt-first on the gravel. The other one saw his friend hit the ground rolling and hopped off. He melted into the crowd. Hitchcock turned to a tall skinny kid with a cigarette in his mouth who was staring at him. He wore a gray sweatshirt with "*Sammamish Track*" in red letters on the chest and a sneer on his face.

"What's going on here, and where are the first two officers?"

"Butt out, piggy," he said with a smirk, looking to his snickering friends for approval. Hitchcock grabbed him by his shirt and jerked him up close. He reeked of beer.

"You're drunk, sonny. If you're here when I come back, I'll arrest you for Minor in Consumption. I'll book your sorry butt into the Youth Center, where the *real* tough kids are. Now—where are the first two officers?"

"Uh—inside. There was a big fight when someone threw pennies and trash at the singer. The pi … I mean the cops broke it up and closed the place."

Hitchcock released him with a shove. "Go home, don't let me see you again tonight, and don't pee your pants as you leave."

He pushed and shoved his way through the crowd. The floor and the stage were littered with trash. Walker and Otis were standing in the middle of the empty dance floor with three handcuffed young male prisoners, talking with the manager and another employee.

"We're okay," Otis said. "We're taking these three in for assault, unlawful consumption and disorderly conduct. They started a small riot by throwing trash and coins at the singer on the stage. A girl in the crowd climbed on the stage and attacked the singer, Jerry Lee Lewis, who threw her off the stage. That started everybody fighting. This one," Otis said, pointing at the tallest and strongest-looking kid," has assault warrants with us; the other two thought they were too tough to be arrested. I could use help getting them through the crowd outside."

"Go on! Jerry Lee Lewis, the "*Great Balls of Fire*" singer—here?" Hitchcock asked.

"Yup, but he left. Let's take these punks to the station."

Batons in one hand, prisoners in the other, they pushed and jabbed their way through the jeering crowd to their cars, where Otis angrily observed his front tires had been slashed. Sherman volunteered to stay with Otis's car until a tow truck arrived.

To keep the fighters apart, two went to the station in Walker's car with Otis; Hitchcock took the third prisoner—a minor who was drunk and in a mood to fight.

"Take these cuffs off and fight me, pig bastards," he told Hitchcock at the station, on the way to the booking room.

Hitchcock shook his head. "Forget it, kid. I've got calls to take."

"You can't put me in the same cell with these two pukes I was arrested with—I'll just finish what I started," the kid sneered.

Hitchcock looked into the other cell. Lajos Csizmadia was there, asleep. *This is a probably a good kid, he just needs a little lesson in respect. I'll help him get it,* he thought.

"Kid, when you were little, did your folks take you to see Santa Claus?" Hitchcock asked with his best straight face.

Surprised by the question, the kid replied "Yeah, so?"

"Well, with your attitude toward these other two guys, it looks like we have no choice but to put you in the other cell with one of Santa's helpers. He's old now, and sometimes, when he drinks, he thinks he really *is* Santa. When he wakes up, if you're nice, he'll tell you stories of the North Pole,"

Csizmadia was snoring on the only bunk in the cell. The kid shook him roughly. "Get up, old man, get up! I want the bunk and I wanna hear about the North Pole."

Hitchcock left the cell area and waited outside the door, staring at his watch counting the seconds. Just as Walker brought a new prisoner into the booking room---

"RRRAAAUGHH!" Csizmadia leaped off the bunk and grabbed the terrified kid by the neck. "So, you t'ink I tell you stories, eh? You want th' bunk, eh? I weel show you, pipe-squeak, who I really am—and what you really are!" The sounds of mayhem followed as the kid tried to resist Csizmadia.

"HEELLP! HELLLP! Officer, please!" The kid started crying. Walker gave his prisoner to the booking officer and went with Hitchcock into the cell area. Csizmadia had the blubbering kid in a headlock, crushing him slowly like a human boa constrictor. Walker stepped in and easily pried Csizmadia's arms off the whimpering kid and handed him to Hitchcock.

"Put me in the other cell! I'll behave," he gasped.

"Not so tough now, are you? Did I hear you say 'please' in that request?" Hitchcock asked sternly.

"Please!" the shaking kid replied.

"Please what?"

"Please, Officer, Sir! Don't let that guy near me!"

Hitchcock put the kid in the same cell with the other two. "The booking officer will get to you boys as soon as possible. No fighting. He'll call *me* if there's any more trouble. The one who causes trouble I will move into Santa's cell."

He returned to his patrol car and radioed Dispatch that he is back in service. Right away he got another call.

"Three Zero Six and Three Zero Four, respond Code Three to a two-car fatality accident on 148th SE at SE 30th. Ambulance and the medical examiner have been called. A-I [accident investigation] units are on the way."

He arrived in three minutes. A mangled red Camaro convertible was on the sidewalk of the southbound lanes of 148th SE. A young man in his twenties was in the driver seat, dead, the top plate of his skull missing as if it had been removed with a power saw, exposing his bright red brains. Firemen from nearby Fire Station#2 were directing traffic and setting out flares.

Jason Allard attended to another man who was hysterical. His car, a yellow Corvette, was wrapped around a metal light standard in the median. Witnesses reported he was drag racing with the driver who died: his brother. Hitchcock and Allard protected the scene and identified witnesses until the traffic division and the medical examiner arrived.

Calls kept pouring in from all over town: family fights, parking lot disturbances, in-progress car prowls, drunk driver arrests, loud music complaints, juvenile drinking parties. There hadn't been time to eat, and by now Hitchcock was hungry. At the moment, he was the only unit not out on a call. He stopped at Charlie's, where Debbie, the winsome blonde bar-maid gave him a left-over leg of fried chicken.

"What time are you off tonight, Roger?" she asked invitingly.

"Dunno, Debbie. From the look of it, maybe never."

He ate in his car to be near the radio. Sure enough, Radio called again: "Radio to Three Zero Six?"

With a sigh of exasperation, he took the mike. *Don't these people ever sleep?*

"Three Zero Six, go."

"What's your 10-20?" [location]

What now? "Just clearing a bar check at Charlie's."

"Respond to a prowler-in-progress in District Five at 12678 SE 29th. Woman alone with her young daughter reports seeing a naked male adult in her back yard. Suspect has climbed over the fence into her neighbor's yard. We have no units available to back you up."

"Tell her I'm minutes away and en route. Keep her on the line until I arrive."

He tossed the drumstick and reached the neighborhood in minutes. He cut his lights and stopped two houses away from the call location.

"Ask the woman to meet me at her front door in thirty seconds. Tell her I will knock on her door twice."

Taking his baton and flashlight, he softly opened his door and eased it closed with a click. There was an eerie quiet in the neighborhood as he hoofed it to the house under moonlight bright enough to read fine print. He rapped twice softly on the door and announced himself in a low voice.

"Police officer!"

A frightened middle-aged woman with her hair in curlers opened the door. She held the door with one hand and a blue steel revolver in the other. It was pointed at the floor.

"I saw a totally naked man standing outside my bedroom window," she said. "I ran to get my gun. I saw him climb over the fence into my neighbor's back yard. They're out for the evening. I just heard a little dog bark, then squeal."

"I'll have a look around. Stay inside."

The caller's backyard was empty. He heard no noises. He let himself through the gate into the back yard next door. The lifeless body of a small white dog was lying on the patio outside the sliding glass door.

He heard a tapping noise in the yard next door. He peeked over the fence. A tall, lean, white male adult, naked except for running shoes, was tapping on a window, peering inside, where lights were on.

Hitchcock vaulted over the six-foot wood fence, completely surprising the prowler, who ran across the yard to the next fence and scaled it like a gymnast.

"Stop! Police! You're under arrest!"

He sprinted across the yard and scaled the fence. The naked prowler reached the other side of the back yard and ran through a gate to the street. Hitchcock pursued. The suspect turned left when he reached the street and lengthened his stride.

Despite the weight of his duty belt, Hitchcock began closing the gap. When he was within a yard of the suspect he reached for the suspect's shoulder, but he wasn't close enough and he was out of breath. His legs were turning to rubber and his lungs were on fire. The suspect began regaining his lead as Hitchcock's stride weakened. Cursed cigarettes!

Desperate, Hitchcock stopped, drew his baton, aimed, and, between gasps, threw it at the suspect's back. The baton hit the pavement before it reached the fleeing suspect. It tumbled end over end between the suspect's feet, causing him to trip and collapse into the juniper bushes at the edge of a front lawn.

He forced his legs and lungs into another run to seize the suspect before he could get up, but he was staggering and gasping for air as he reached the suspect who struggled to get on his feet.

Hitchcock sized the suspect up for a knockout punch. He was the same height as himself; slightly over six feet, athletically built; a bit under two hundred pounds. The suspect was fit, but he was at least ten years older than Hitchcock. He should go down easily if his punch was on target.

He stumbled on the shrubbery as he reached the suspect and almost fell in the bushes. The suspect was standing. He was obviously hurt; probably because he was naked except for his shoes. There was nothing for Hitchcock to grab.

"Police! Stop right there!" Hitched said between gasps as he tripped over thin branches trying to find solid footing. "You're under arrest!"

The suspect stepped back, about to turn and run. There was no time for Hitchcock to plant his feet for a punch.

Hitchcock was desperate; it was now or never. He fired a long, overhand right cross, from the shoulder, putting his weight behind it---a sure knockout punch, aimed at the tip of the suspect's jaw.

Lack of good footing caused him to hit the suspect's mouth instead of his jaw. It sent him flying backward into the junipers. Hitchcock lunged forward to seize the suspect by the arm, but he tripped on the shrubbery and fell, landing close to the suspect. He was too winded to get to his feet.

The predator staggered to his feet without a word, stepping back out of the officer's reach, holding his jaw. Shaken by the punch, he wobbled away, his stride became a jog that kept gaining speed. Hitchcock tried to stand up but couldn't. He watched the naked suspect running full-tilt until he vanished. Moments later he heard a car start up about a block away and leave.

Hitchcock knelt on both knees in the shrubs, dejected, out of breath. Chunks of fried chicken came out of him as he vomited; gasping for air and hating himself for smoking, a habit he picked up in the Army.

Within seconds the headlights of Sherman's patrol car found him. His uniform pants and shirt were torn, and he was nauseated. Sherman helped him to his feet.

"You okay?"

"No," he said, still panting.

Sherman drove Hitchcock back to his car. "I'll be busy here for a bit. The neighborhood woke up and is in an uproar over this."

Hitchcock remained in his cruiser at the scene, until he had written a detailed report and made a pencil sketch of the suspect's face.

His mind was racing. He already felt responsible for the suspect's future attacks because he failed to arrest him. *This guy is out of control. Anybody who risks running around in neighborhoods with no clothes on and kills a dog for barking at him is ready to start killing people. He can't stop. He'll keep going until we catch him,* he mentally concluded. He cringed at the thought of reading news stories about the trail of victims that were to come.

Calls kept pouring in right up until 4 a.m. The nausea had subsided by the time Hitchcock refueled his cruiser, and as he walked into the station, he tossed his smokes in the trash.

CHAPTER 2

DEATH OF A HIT MAN

Monday, 7 a.m.

The captain of detectives, Dennis Holland, was at his desk early. Within minutes, two of his men, plus detectives from the King County Sheriff's Office, would be meeting to discuss the murder of hit man Colin Wilcox.

The evidence that detectives found in Wilcox's car after obtaining a search warrant, plus the murder of Wilcox immediately after his release from jail, erased any doubt that organized crime has been pursuing interests in the suburbs.

Holland looked forward to meeting Hitchcock. He had been hearing of the young officer's arrests for weeks, and he was impressed by the quality of his reports.

Hitchcock awakened to dog breath and Jamie woofing in his ear, wanting to be let out. Having been allowed to go home early Sunday night to be ready for the meeting, he felt rested and ready. He shook his head in disgust at the usual cold Northwest drizzle when he opened the back door for Jamie.

He checked his watch---he had to be quick. Reheated stale coffee, two hastily scrambled eggs, hit the shower. Pressed blue jeans, the new Pendleton wool shirt Rhonda gave him, gun, badge and jacket.

He was barely acquainted with any of the detectives except in passing, let alone the captain who headed the division or anyone from the King County Sheriff's Office. It was 8 a.m. when he walked into the detectives' office.

"Good morning, Roger. I'm glad to finally meet you. I'm Dennis Holland, the captain around here, and these are the detectives who served the search warrant on Wilcox's car: Joe Small and Larry Meyn. Over here, meet King County Detective Captain Ned Williams and Detective Roy Thomas."

He noticed notepads, thick stacks of reports, photographs and unsealed evidence envelopes on the conference table as he shook hands with everyone and sat down.

Captain Holland began: "Roger, our purpose here today is to talk with you about your arrest of Wilcox. We're looking for anything you may not have disclosed in your report. We have learned that Wilcox was an out-of-town hit man, a professional. He was a suspect in several murders between Spokane and Chicago. He was paroled from Walla Walla earlier this year, where he served time for manslaughter. Detectives Small and Meyn have been working on this since Wilcox was arrested. I defer to Joe to lay out the facts."

Detective Small was in his early 30's. Except for the way he wore his blond hair in the longish style of the 70s' he resembled the square-jawed boxer in the Sunday newspaper comics, Joe Palooka. "The evidence we found in Wilcox's car indicates he was hired for a mission that involved Charlie's Place," Small said. "He had a police scanner set to monitor both of our radio frequencies; binoculars; and a notebook in which he had written the shift hours of the

Patrol Division, the call signs and the times that the Eastgate units on night shift made bar-checks. From the receipts for meals and lodging we found in his car, we learned he conducted surveillance on us for about four weeks.

"He surveilled *us*?" Hitchcock asked.

"That's right. Whoever hired him has deep pockets. By the end of four weeks he had reason to be certain no one would be checking Charlie's on a weeknight until at least 9 p.m. ----He knew your pattern."

Hitchcock was too stunned to say anything. Small continued.

"Wilcox also recorded the descriptions and plate numbers of officers' personal vehicles, when they arrived for work, and when they left. He had *us* under surveillance. He sat in our parking lot for weeks, watching and listening to shifts rotate."

"And nobody even noticed him," Hitchcock said.

"That's right---shame on us," said Detective Small.

"Do we know what this was about? Who hired him?"

"The answer to both your questions, Roger, is that we don't know. He ate at The Great Wall eight times over the four-week period before you arrested him. Paid cash every time. The Great Wall is the only Bellevue business we found receipts for. It's rare to find a criminal that is so meticulous."

"Not good," said Hitchcock.

"He was well-funded, and we found no indication he was funding himself by committing other crimes like robbery because none of the current suspect descriptions match Wilcox, with or without his disguise," Detective Small added.

"Hold on," said Hitchcock. "Wilcox had no wallet on him and only a few bucks in his pocket when we arrested him. I was wondering how he was supporting himself. Besides the receipts, how do you know he was well-funded?"

"Good question, Roger," Detective Small said. "We found a key for a safe deposit box at a bank in Issaquah in his car. We got a search warrant and found over three thousand dollars in small bills in it."

"Where was he staying?"

"The old Alpine Motel on Highway 10 in Issaquah. There were two gaps of several days each in his stays there; where he was during those times is unknown. We found receipts for the false beard and the wig—from a shop on Skid Row in Seattle—purchased two days before you arrested him. The shop owner remembered he was picky and paid cash."

"What about the gun he had?" Hitchcock asked.

"The lab identified Wilcox's prints on the Browning Hi-Power, the loaded thirteen-round magazine in the gun, and the other magazine in the glove box which was also loaded," Detective Meyn said.

"Wilcox must have worn gloves to handle the ammunition--no prints on any of the cartridges in the magazines were found. The feds traced the gun from the factory to a sporting goods store in Spokane in '67. It was sold privately two months later. The original owner says he sold it a year later. It probably changed hands several times since then. It was never reported stolen. How Wilcox got it is for us to find out, as the feds have no interest in the case. "

"The only two businesses in our City that Wilcox went to that we know of were Charlie's and The Great Wall," Small said. "We could find no connection between them or their owners. Larry and I interviewed and showed Wilcox's mug shot to the owner of The Great Wall, Juju Kwan; she insists she never saw Wilcox in her place or anywhere else. She apparently doesn't know we have her receipts that say she is wrong, if not lying. Wilcox was there. We talked to the waitresses and bartenders there—they all claimed, through Juju, of course, that they don't understand English. Since Juju's employees are all Asian immigrants, it could be they have a cultural fear of the police; we can't be sure."

"You should ask Juju if she would mind having an interpreter from U.S. Customs come with you next time," the county detective said. "Odds are her workers are slaves she brought here illegally."

"I should have thought of that at the time, but I didn't. Neither of us did," Joe Small said.

Captain Holland continued.

"We spoke with Wally Evans, the owner of Charlie's, who made a point of telling us how much he appreciates you, but it was the same story—says he never saw or heard of Wilcox before this."

Noticing Hitchcock's dismay, Small asked, "Hey, Roger, you still with us?"

"Not really. I'm feeling really stupid, making my routine so predictable."

Small shook his head. "It's not a perfect world, and in police work, all's well that ends well. If you hadn't changed your pattern by going to Charlie's when you did, who knows how many people would have been hurt or killed. We want you in on this because you were the key player in upsetting their plans and District Six is your beat."

"Am I at risk now?"

"The best answer I can give you," Captain Holland said, "is probably. Consider the facts as we know them now: Wilcox, a known hit man from out-of-town, shows up. His expenses are fully paid while he spends weeks surveilling the police department. Two nights in a row, Wilcox goes to Charlie's right after he leaves The Great Wall. Each time he goes there just before eight o'clock, when he is sure that there is a shift change going on, so no officers are on the streets to respond to an emergency. He believes, from watching and listening to you on the radio, that he has about an hour to do his thing and escape on the freeway before you can be there. Because you will be checking buildings elsewhere at the start of your shift. He is armed with a gun that has a high capacity magazine, a knife, and he's disguised.

"His plans were aborted when you unexpectedly changed your routine and arrived early. He wound up in jail. Wilcox and those who sent him must have concluded that someone informed on them. Wilcox is mysteriously bailed out of jail and murdered to ensure his silence."

"So, you're saying there is no way to know if I am at risk," Hitchcock said.

"Correct," Holland said. "We have taken this case as far as the time Wilcox's body was discovered out in the county. The murder is a King County case but we are still pursuing what the mission was and who hired Wilcox. You should assume you are at risk."

Ned Williams was a twelve-year veteran of the King County Sheriff's Office. A quiet, easy-going sort, investigating organized crime was his personal sub-specialty as he climbed the ranks.

"First off," Williams began, "the manner of Wilcox's death is typical of East Coast mob execution. It is extremely rare out here. The body was intended to be found as a warning." He shoved a stack of enlarged photos across the table to Hitchcock.

"Wilcox was bound and walked to a secluded spot in the woods about twenty yards from the road, then shot once in the base of his skull with a .22," Captain Williams said. 'The body was found in a sitting position, back against a tree. The medical examiner estimates the death occurred two weeks before the body was discovered. It was badly deteriorated from inclement weather and animal activity. The toxicology report stated a detectable level of barbiturate was still present in the organs. We think they doped him up before they took him to the execution spot"

Hitchcock looked through the photos. He would never have recognized Wilcox. Much of his face had been eaten away by wild animals; probably coyotes and raccoons.

"How long after his release from jail do you think Wilcox died?" he asked.

"It appears he was killed almost immediately after his release," Williams replied. "Probably because his failed mission and arrest made him too much of a liability to whoever hired him, so he was taken out as a form of damage control. Investigation into Wilcox's release is ongoing, so I can't comment further on it now.

"It comes down to this: organized crime figures in Seattle are peaceable compared to their counter--parts in other parts of the country. They own topless bars and peep shows and launder the money through real estate investments like low income apartment complexes. They live quietly in nice suburbs like Bellevue and typically don't dirty their own backyard. They understand and accept that they are being watched."

"It's your turn, now, Roger, we would like to know what led you to alter your patrol routine so that you and Ira Walker went to Charlie's first?" Captain Holland asked.

Hitchcock shrugged. "Just gut instinct I've had as long as I can remember. I learned to listen to it in 'Nam. It's how I stayed alive. What Wally Evans, the owner of Charlie's Place, told me about this strange guy the previous night stuck with me. Because the next day would be payday for a lot of local folks who regularly go to Charlie's on payday, I had a nagging feeling he would be back, so I changed my routine out of instinct I asked Walker to go with me."

"Anything else? What happened when you got there?" Holland asked.

"As we walked toward the back door a strange guy stepped out, looked at us and ran back inside. Wally Evans was behind the bar and obviously afraid. He indicated non-verbally to me that the man was hiding in the ladies' room. I figured we had either interrupted a felony in progress or there was a fugitive hiding there. After I arrested him I learned Wilcox had locked the front door from the inside to prevent escape. I think he was about to lock the rear door when we arrived unexpectedly, and he panicked."

"So, what are your conclusions now?" Captain Williams asked.

"I'm new to this, but whatever was planned, the intention was to do something so drastic it would break Charlie's so that no one would go there again. Maybe someone in Wally's past or the previous owner has it in for him. Maybe it's connected to drugs."

"Most crime is centered on drugs nowadays," said Detective Meyn.

"Last week a biker from way up in Granite Falls was involved in an accident on I-90, seconds after I saw him leaving The Great Wall, which had been closed all that night. I helped the state trooper at the scene, who later told me the biker's blood tested positive for cocaine which he said he got at the Chinese place there. There's only one such place in Eastgate. "

Captain Williams nodded in agreement. "Juju Kwan is certainly a suspect in this, and it's a safe bet the people behind Wilcox are aware of you because you upset their plans. Although it's rare that cops who nail bad guys by the rules are targeted for retribution, we don't know who is behind this; you should have eyes in the back of your head."

Hitchcock started to leave when Captain Williams spoke again.

"One more thing I almost forgot, Roger. In the process of investigation, we learned that Wallace Evans, the owner of Charlie's, did hard time in Illinois for fraud and embezzlement; a federal charge of racketeering was dropped. He was paroled in '67, came out here in '68. He and a partner named Louie Adragna, also an ex-con, bought the tavern with cash. Where the cash came from is a mystery. After a year, Adragna disappeared. He's still missing two years later—so make that two mysteries."

CHAPTER 3

BUCKWHEATS, BACON AND A SPY

Hitchcock's head was spinning as he left the meeting. Wally Evans a convicted felon? That, as much as anything said in the meeting, was a shock. He felt embarrassed, like a blundering novice. *How could I have not sensed that Wally is a convict? It explains how he recognized Wilcox for what he was—a fellow convict. How stupid I must look!*

Not only did it bother him that Wally Evans must have a condescending view of him and the other officers for not knowing about his criminal past, but what about hitman Colin Wilcox? What must Wilcox have thought of a police department whose station he could put under surveillance for *four weeks* and not get caught or even questioned? No wonder Wilcox thought his mission would be easy!

He needed to eat the slices of humble pie that were in front of him, but not give up. Never. He would take a step back, clear his head and move forward.

Firing up his metallic gold El Camino, he tuned in the radio to KVI, 570 on the AM dial. It had been months since his sleep schedule permitted him to listen to "Robert E. Lee" Hardwick in the morning, his favorite radio personality.

Ahead of Hardwick was the local news, announcing a coalition of students that was organizing in Seattle to protest the spreading of the war into Laos. Disgusted, Hitchcock turned the radio off. He left the station, his mind swirling too much to pay attention to his driving. When his mind came back to the present, he found himself parking in front of the Pancake Corral.

Ada, the dark-haired one of the owners' two daughters was at the cash register when he walked in. She seated him in Allie's Malloy's section and brought him coffee. "Allie will be right here," she said with a knowing grin.

He was adding creamer to his coffee when a woman's voice behind him said "Morning, Roger. Are you on a change of schedule?" He turned. It was Allie. Her feminine aura, warm smile, the musical lilt in her voice and her woman scent erased the stress from a morning filled with upsetting news.

"Just for today. How's your little one?"

"Baby teeth on the way in," she said with a sigh of exasperation. "Costing mama her sleep. Just four more hours before I can go home, and hopefully take a nap. What can I get you? Coffee, of course."

"Coffee, yes, and buckwheat pancakes, a side of bacon, and a small slice of time with you when your shift ends today."

She smiled broadly, hands on her hips. "What? That's it? No eggs? Just buckwheat, bacon and... ? No dancing girls to keep you entertained while you wait? Hmmm. This isn't the Roger I know."

He liked her sense of humor. It was his turn to smile. "No dancers today, just the morning paper and a little time to talk with you later."

She handed him yesterday's Seattle Times and the morning Seattle Post Intelligencer. The Times featured a photo of a group of ratty-looking UW student protestors holding a sign that read '"Student Power End the War." He put the Times aside and opened the sports section of the PI to Royal Brougham's column about the Huskies' Rose Bowl prospects.

He really didn't want the paper to read; he used it to peek over the top to watch Allie work. Tired as she was, Allie worked efficiently, cheering even the grumpiest customers, checking on their orders, refilling their coffee, calling many by name.

Her everything-in-the-right-place figure and golden hair in a ponytail delighted him as well as the other male customers, but he found himself delighting just as much in what he saw of her character.

As poor as her car indicated she was, Allie was cheerful; as attractive as she was, she avoided dating in order to be a mom to her infant son. He admired her transparency and selflessness; she was a rarity, a beautiful woman without guile. She brought his order with a note: *"Nick's on Park Row at 2:30."*

He ate quickly. She met him at the cash register. "OK. Nick's, it is, but before that I need to borrow your car."

"What? Why?"

"Police business; today only. I need another car they won't recognize me in," he fibbed.

"When will you bring it back?"

"In about two hours, I promise."

Five-foot-one Allie squinted suspiciously up at him. "This sure is unusual of you, Roger Hitchcock. What's going on?"

"Can I have the key?" he asked, holding out his hand, struggling to keep a straight face.

She left and came back and handed him the key. "Two hours, I'm holding you to it."

Yeah, how I wish you would 'hold me to it,' he thought. "Don't worry," he said with a grin.

Allie's Toyota was a sturdy little beater in need of some TLC. It started with the slightest turn of the key. He noticed a silver sedan of American make leave the gas station parking lot next door as he headed north to the downtown.

He went about his business, keeping an eye out for the silver car, which followed him at a distance. He lost sight of it when he withdrew cash from his savings at National Bank of Commerce, went to Firestone Tire for all new tires on Allie's car, then had the engine tuned, oil changed and tank filled at Barney and Al's Chevron, a stone's throw from the Corral. It was 1:55 when he strolled back into the Corral, gave Allie the key and left.

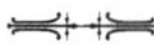

At 2:26 p.m. he was waiting for Allie in a booth at Nick's BBQ. It was empty except for himself and Nick, who was preparing a roast for the dinner crowd. He got to his feet when she came in.

"Roger! You didn't have to do that! Why?" She exclaimed.

He shrugged. "It's your honorability," he said.

"Honora-what?"

"Honorability."

"Whatever, but I can't accept this. I can't afford to pay you back!"

"No strings attached."

Yeah, with SO many women after you, you never need to attach strings to anything you do. No chance for someone like me, she thought.

"Nobody's ever done anything like this for me before. I mean, really. I ..."

"Let's order something before we talk."

During the next half-hour Allie poured out her life story: a local girl from a working-class family, she met the father of her baby while she was a freshman at the UW and working at the downtown Frederick & Nelson store as a waitress. Within a month she was pregnant and he married her in a civil ceremony. His parents didn't approve when they found out. Under their pressure he filed for divorce the week the baby was born. After the divorce was final, his parents went to court to get full custody, claiming she was an unfit mother. The judge saw through them and awarded full custody to her and assigned child support and maintenance responsibilities with limited visitation to the father.

"Why didn't his parents like you?"

"My background, I guess; a construction worker's daughter. Dad died of a heart attack four years ago. My mom's a Safeway cashier. We're from Renton—too blue-collar for rich folks like them. They were ashamed of me."

"Well, being the curious type I am, I watched him leave your place after our meeting and ran the plate on the Benz he drove. You can really pick 'em—McAuliffe—one of Washington's oldest families—and the richest. Timber, real estate, politics—two past governors, and a state senator. They own chunks of downtown Seattle. Rumor is that Ian McAuliffe, your ex father-in-law, is politically far to the left, a suspected communist sympathizer."

"Richard never talked about his parents or politics with me. Like his parents, he was ashamed of me when I became pregnant, because I didn't fit in and never would. Richard has never worked; he lives on an allowance from his parents. They threatened to cut him off if he didn't divorce me. The child support is based on what they told the court his allowance was—they all lied to the court regarding the amount—so what I get is pitifully small, but I need it. It's like pulling teeth every month. He's always late and makes excuses."

"What about this 'Jim Reynolds' guy you told me about? Any more from him?"

"He called last weekend; wanted to meet me for coffee but I turned him down, told him my son had the sniffles. Before I could end the call, he went off on another tirade about using violence to right the wrongs in this evil country of ours."

As Allie spoke, Hitchcock noticed the man sitting in the silver sedan facing them in the Firestone Tire parking lot across the street, the same car that followed him when he took Allie's car from the Pancake Corral to the tire store.

"I want to know every time he calls you—right away. And don't agree to see him any more until I figure out who he is and what's going on." He handed her a slip of paper. "Here are my phone numbers; home and work."

He kept his eyes off the sedan across the street as he walked her to her car. She got in and cranked the window down. "Thank you so much for helping me, Roger. It means a lot to have a friend like you."

"We'll stay in touch," he replied casually, making sure not to glance at the occupied car across the street.

He went back inside Nick's. Through the window he watched the gray sedan begin following Allie. He ran to his El Camino and tailed the car that was tailing Allie to her apartment.

A balding, middle-aged man got out of the silver sedan. He had a camera with a long lens in his hand. He crept in bent-over fashion among the parked cars to a position behind bushes at the edge of the apartment parking lot. He knelt and began snapping pictures with a camera of Allie ascending the stairs to her apartment. Hitchcock slipped out of his El Camino and approached him from behind.

"Hey you, what are you doing?"

The man was startled. "Uh … nothing, really. Who's asking?"

"I am. Hey, that's some camera you got there! Pentax Spotmatic, eh?" Hitchcock snatched it from his hand, cranked the film winder until it stopped, opened the back, pocketed the film roll, and handed the camera back.

"Hey! What the---what do you think you're doing?"

"Wrong question. The right question is what are *you* doing out here, hiding in the bushes, following and taking pictures of the young woman who just went up those stairs."

The man's face reddened. "That is *none* of your business. Give me the film back and I won't call the police."

Hitchcock flashed his badge. "I *am* the police. We have an ordinance in this town called vagrancy—defined as wandering and prowling. What I've seen you doing fits the bill. You have two choices: start talking. If your purpose is legit, I'll return your film. If you refuse to talk I'll take you in and impound your car. Pick one."

"I'm a private investigator," the spy said with a sigh, "licensed in Seattle. I have that woman under surveillance for a client. It's a civil matter. That's all I can say." He produced a license from his wallet. It was issued to Tobias Olson by the City of Seattle; it was current. "Now give me my film back."

"Not so fast. You could be just saying that. Maybe you're not Tobias Olson; maybe you're a stalker. Who's your client and why is the woman under surveillance?"

"My client's identity is confidential. You ought to know that. Now give me that film!" he demanded angrily.

"Nope. I'll forward this to my supervisor to let the City Prosecutor decide what to do. Of course, before your film is released, in addition to who your client is, they'll have to determine if you're licensed to conduct business in the City of Bellevue. Are you? "

He grimaced with bitter anger as he got into his car., "You will hear from my attorney about this, and you can go to hell, Officer!"

"Already been there—twice."

The private spy left, and Hitchcock looked at the film roll in his hand. *Why is a private dick spying on Allie? I'll take the film to our photo lab for developing,* he decided. As he turned to leave. he noticed a small, middle-aged woman with a blue scarf over her head standing at the bottom of the stair case, watching him. Her resemblance to Allie was striking. *She must be Allie's mom and saw me confront Olson,* he thought.

He stopped at the city's photo lab, where he gave city photographer Frank Kilmer the film and the story. "I'll have it ready for you in a couple days, Roger," he promised. "Got two deadlines to meet first."

CHAPTER 4
THE REAPER'S MAN

Dispatch had a call waiting for him as he radioed himself in service:

> "See the manager at the Cedar Grove Apartments, 1510 148th SE regarding a D.O.A. [Dead On Arrival] The victim's parents are standing by. A detective has been called and the medical examiner is on the way. Code One."

He had been to this low-income apartment complex before on domestic violence, car prowls and runaway juvenile calls. The manager, a retired school teacher named Toby, was waiting outside his office. He appeared relieved to see it was Hitchcock who came to the call.

"Thanks for coming so quickly, Roger. A girl named Janine, was renting Unit 11 upstairs for about two months; she was a student at Bellevue Community College. Her parents have been paying her rent. They stopped hearing from her so they drove up from Olympia. The apartment was locked. I let them in. Looks like an overdose."

They went into the rental office where Toby introduced Hitchcock to a middle--aged couple. They were in shock and struggling to hold their grief in check. He went with them to Unit 11, where, in a sparsely furnished one-bedroom apartment, the naked body of a slightly overweight young woman was lying supine on the living room floor, her legs spread wide apart, a hypodermic needle lying between her thighs.

The strong odor of decaying flesh hung in the air like a low cloud. Purplish blotches of advanced postmortem lividity were everywhere on her body; they blended with what appeared to Hitchcock to be bruises on her wrists and arms. Scars from needle marks were visible on the inside of her left arm; fresh needle marks were on the insides of her thighs, close to her vagina.

Her mouth and her eyes were open and dark. The thermostat read sixty-six degrees. Hitchcock lifted an arm by the hand to check for rigor mortis, though he already knew it was long gone. Looking at the lividity and the room temperature, he guessed the time of death at about two days ago.

The girl's mother handed Hitchcock a note. "This is our daughter, Janine. We found this lying next to her, Officer. It's Janine's writing," she said.

It was handwritten, addressed from the victim to a man named Willie in which she expressed in the crudest terms the sexual favors she would bestow on him when he got out of prison.

"Ma'am, I am so sorry for your loss. I know this is extremely hard for you, but I need you and your husband to tell me everything about your daughter, as much as you can, especially who her friends were," Hitchcock explained as gently as he could.

The father stood in a corner of the nearly vacant apartment, stoic, hands behind his back, jaw clenched; he looked like he was ready to explode. The mother shook her head, doing her best to hold her grief in check in order to help her daughter one last time.

"We're a Christian family, Officer. Janine is—was—the youngest of our four kids," the mother said. "She was always the family rebel. At home in Olympia she rejected our principles at an early age, ran with the wrong crowd. In her teens, she experimented with drugs and sex with older boys. First it was marijuana, but soon she was into LSD after listening to that Timothy Leary fellow. She almost died once when she overdosed on heroin.

"After she completed a year in drug rehab we helped her enroll in college up here, thinking a change in environment would be good. About a week ago, we stopped hearing from her. We checked the college; she had enrolled but they had no record of her attending classes. When she didn't answer her phone, we came up here tonight after my husband got off work to find out what is going on and why...."

She bit her lower lip, holding back tears as she struggled for the right words. "We've been down this road with her before. We always ... we feared ... it might ... our Janine. Sick ... terrible. How could this happen to us?"

"The car we bought for her is missing, Officer," the father said. "I've checked the parking lot; it's gone."

Ian Barstow, one of the Medical Examiner's investigators, arrived. He already had one body in the back of his station wagon; a man's hand protruded from under the green sheet covering. When Detective Small showed up, Hitchcock re-contacted the manager.

"Toby, tell me about this girl, who her friends or visitors were. What happened to her car?"

"I should've called you, Roger, but I hesitated. Suspicious activity, I'd call it, but nothing definite. Now, of course, I wish I had called."

"Suspicious activity?"

"Yeah, well there was always this older--looking black guy coming to her apartment, always bringing different men with him. Drives an older white Lincoln, sometimes a chunky blonde woman is his driver. Other times Janine would leave in her car—a green Maverick—and come back followed by one or two men in another car.

"Then, day before yesterday, the black guy came here with the blonde girl in the white Lincoln. About a half-hour later I saw the blonde leaving alone in the Lincoln. A few minutes later the same black guy drove away in Janine's Maverick. He was alone. Wish now I had called," Toby said, ruefully shaking his head. "Didn't want folks thinkin' I'm prejudiced. Still, I shoulda called."

Hitchcock returned to the apartment and reported the manager's information to Detective Small. "The girl's dad has signed a stolen report. Is it OK to put the car description on the air now?"

"Do it," Small said. "Let's get the guy. The Medical Examiner, Barstow, says this is his second OD in Bellevue tonight, and both look like heroin."

"Second? When was the first?"

"A couple hours ago, before you came on shift. Larry Meyn got called out on that one. For a Monday, it's been busy."

Hitchcock returned to his cruiser and keyed his mike. "Three Zero Six, Radio. I have stolen vehicle information to broadcast."

"Three Zero Six, go."

"To all units—we have a signed stolen report on a green 1967 Ford Maverick four-door, bearing Washington license Ocean Paul Adam Six Three Seven. Vehicle has a crumpled left front fender. Last seen leaving the Cedar Grove Apartments 48 hours ago, driven by an unidentified Negro male adult, described as older--looking. The driver is also a suspect in the DOA at this complex. Consider armed and dangerous if located."

Hitchcock remained at the scene. It began raining when he helped Ian Barstow lug the gurney carrying Janine Collins's sheet-draped body downstairs to his station wagon.

"Heroin's spreading into the suburbs now; two in your town tonight already," Barstow said. "This new stuff from Vietnam is more powerful than the usual stuff. Most addicts here can't handle it. Many of 'em are dying. You should see what it's like in Seattle."

Hitchcock cleared the scene and headed to the Hilltop Inn, next to the freeway and the airport, where pimps, prostitutes and drug dealers did business at the bar and the rooms upstairs. He switched radio channels to Records on F2 and began running license plates in the parking lot for outstanding warrants.

Right away there was a hit on a white '65 Cadillac Fleetwood for armed robbery and unlawful possession of a firearm. The wanted subject was Ronald Davis, NMA, DOB 7-8-45, height six-feet-two, weight one-eighty.

"Received. Please confirm warrants while I switch back to F1." He switched channels and keyed his mike. "Three Zero Six requesting backup at the Hilltop Inn. Unoccupied vehicle with active felony warrants. Code One."

He walked around the Cadillac and shone his flashlight into the interior. It was empty. He parked at a distance while he waited for confirmation of the warrants and the arrival of a backup unit. Then the radio crackled:

"Three Zero Six, check out reports in District Eight of a woman screaming for help, area of 149th and SE 14th. We've had three calls so far; unknown situation. Code Two."

He arrived in the neighborhood in four minutes. A middle-aged man in a sweater and khaki pants was on the street, waving to him to pull over.

"Woman screaming somewhere up there, around the corner," the man pointed, "sounds like she's saying something about her son." A woman's wailing cut the air. "There it is again. If it's the Fowler boy, it'll be bad."

He drove up another block and rounded the corner. He saw a woman he knew—Barbara Fowler—the mother of a childhood friend. She was hysterical. *This has to be about Randy,* he thought. He rolled up to her and got out.

"Thank God it's you, Roger! Randy's overdosed and I think he's dead!"

"Where is he?"

"In the house! Quick!"

There wasn't time to call in his arrival. He bailed out of his cruiser and ran toward the rundown little rambler.

"Why didn't you call us from your house, Mrs. Fowler? It would've saved time."

"Phone company turned off the service yesterday—my check bounced," she said, panting and crying.

He dashed through the front door ahead of Barbara Fowler into the cluttered living room where his childhood friend lay on the couch; eyes closed, skin cool and turning blue, no pulse. He grabbed Randy by the front of his shirt and dragged him to the floor and began chest compressions and mouth-to-mouth resuscitation. After two minutes Randy began coughing.

Hitchcock scooped his emaciated friend into his arms and carried him to his patrol car. "Quick, Mrs. Fowler, open that door and get in the back. I'll hand him to you. Keep his head elevated, in your lap so he can breathe. We're going to the ER. There's no time to lose!"

He laid Randy on the back seat with his head toward his mother's lap and closed the door. He fired up his cruiser, flipped on the overhead emergency light and keyed the mike.

"Three Zero Six, Radio, I have revived an overdose victim and am transporting him with his mother to Overlake ER. Code

Three. Advise them I am on my way and to be standing by for my arrival."

"Radio to Three Zero Six, you do not want a Flintoff's for the transport, correct?"

"Affirmative. Subject wasn't breathing and had no pulse when I arrived. I gave him CPR. He's breathing now but we can't wait."

"Ten-Four. We'll notify Overlake ER."

He flipped the switch for the siren and weaved around traffic through intersections, west on Lake Hills Boulevard, north on 148th Avenue, hitting speeds of seventy, and eighty, with frequent braking and lane-changing through traffic on the way to the straight three-mile stretch of NE 8th Street to the ER. Barbara Fowler went into shrieking hysterics when violent convulsions gripped her son. "Don't die, son! Don't die! Please! Oh God, don't let Randy die, please, please!"

The volume of Barbara Fowler's desperate pleading with the Almighty for her son's life competed with the wailing siren, as Randy retched, convulsed and vomited on her lap.

"I'm getting us there as quickly as I can; keep talking to him!" Hitchcock shouted to her over the siren.

Cars heading in both directions pulled aside as the black-and-white, red light and siren in full operation, reached speeds of over ninety on the open, flat stretches of NE 8th Street, slowing at hillcrests and busting red signals at intersections.

A nurse and two orderlies waited under the metal canopy at the ER entrance when they arrived. Hitchcock opened the rear door. Randy was turning blue again. The hospital team laid him on a gurney and whisked him inside, his despairing mother following behind, unmindful of her son's vomit on her dress.

The orderlies wheeled Randy into the Intensive Care Unit and closed the doors, leaving Barbara outside in the hallway.

"Randy's safe now, Mrs. Fowler. We got him here alive, and what happens next is out of our hands. Maybe now you can tell me what happened," Hitchcock told her. "Let's step into this waiting room where we can talk."

"Damn right, I'll tell you everything, Roger. I've known you since you were a kid. I have fond memories of you and Randy in Little League, when your dad was the coach, and you and Randy were friends. But Randy wasn't like you; he never could stay out of trouble.

"Randy got into pot, then cocaine. Thought we had it under control until last spring when he met that pusher, that black bastard from Seattle who got him hooked on heroin.

"Suddenly Randy, who never had money of his own and couldn't keep a job, had money all the time, yet no work. Wouldn't say where it came from, but I knew; from the needle marks on his arms and how much weight he was losing, it was obvious. Now this. I have a gun, and if I see Tyrone again, Roger, I'll kill him and you can arrest me."

"Tyrone? Tell me about Tyrone."

Barbara wiped her tears again. "He's colored. I hate him. I know you had Negro friends from your boxing days, but, forgive me—I'm an angry and bitter mom. Tyrone Hatch is his name. He's in his forties; a pusher and a pimp. He offered Randy free heroin to get my daughter Connie hooked; you know what he wanted her for. He threatened me when I stepped in and stopped it."

"How did he threaten you?"

"Pointed a pistol at my head, in my own house, in front of my kids, said he'd kill me. But I didn't back down—*he* did. I called his bluff. "Go ahead—shoot me. You can't have my daughter," I said. He's a coward---he left without saying anything."

"What happened today?"

"Today, he came by and gave Randy some of this new heroin he says is from Vietnam. I thought Randy was dead. That's when

I started screaming. He was blue. Then you showed up and knew what to do to save him. Our family owes you for saving him, Roger. I hear you were a medic in the Army."

"Mrs. Fowler, how can I find Tyrone? Where does he live?"

"I don't know. Randy can probably tell you. Tyrone always shows up unannounced."

"*How* does he show up; in a car, with someone, or what?"

"Always in a big white Cadillac. It's not a new one, but the one I saw him in this last time was different, a small car--a fairly new Ford—a Maverick, I think."

"Was that car green?" Hitchcock asked.

Barbara looked surprised. "Why yes, it was. It was driven by a young heavy-set white girl with short, bleach-blonde hair. Do you know Tyrone?"

A balding middle-aged man wearing hospital scrubs and a face mask around his neck, entered the room. "Mrs. Fowler?" he asked. Barbara nodded. "I'm Dr. Collier. Randy is out of danger for now. He's lucky to be alive. We've stabilized his heart rate and sedated him and got IVs in him. We'll need to keep him under observation in Intensive Care for twenty-four to forty-eight hours. He will need treatment after he is released. A case worker will come in to get information from you, especially his drug history."

After the case worker met with Barbara Fowler, Hitchcock took her home. "Show me Randy's room," he asked.

"Absolutely. I'll even help you search," she said.

In minutes, he found a stash of five balloons filled with white powder, hypodermic needles, a burnt spoon and a short length of surgical tubing in the nightstand in Randy's room.

"Look what I found in his closet," Barbara said, holding in one hand a white envelope stuffed with ten, twenty and fifty-dollar bills, and a plastic baggie filled with what Hitchcock recognized as marijuana.

Barbara began crying and shook her head in despair. "I don't know what to do, Roger. This is destroying my family."

"Actually, you're in a position to help a lot, Mrs. Fowler," Hitchcock said as he packaged the drugs and cash in separate evidence envelopes.

"How?"

"Help me find Tyrone Hatch. I want him off the streets. Randy and Connie must know how to reach him. Second, you can be my eyes and ears for others like Hatch. It will save lives; like Randy, Connie and Jim."

"Count me in. Soon as I get my phone service back I'll leave messages for you."

Hitchcock sealed and labeled the evidence and placed it with state crime lab drug analysis request forms into the evidence room. He handed his completed report to Sergeant Breen.

"Nice work!" Breen said. "You've not only gotten a lead on who our bad guy is, but you literally saved someone's life tonight; must be a good feeling. Keep up this kind of work and you'll be taking my job before you know it."

Hitchcock grinned. "Nah, I like it right where I am. I'm having too much fun now. Babysitting would ruin it."

Breen laughed. "While you were busy I ran a check on Tyrone Hatch. He's got a long rap sheet that includes an outstanding felony warrant for illegal firearm possession, in addition to drug-related offenses and weapons charges, including promoting prostitution, all occurring in Seattle. I confirmed the warrant with County and requested Hatch's mugshots for our bulletins. Dispatch broadcasted the descriptions of Hatch and both cars."

"From what I learned tonight, this guy Hatch is a drug pusher selling a new strain of heroin from Vietnam that is stronger than the usual stuff. We had two deaths here just tonight, and almost a third. The M.E. investigator told me addicts have been dying in Seattle for some time now; it's new only here. Plus, Hatch is apparently also a pimp," Hitchcock said.

"I'll add that to our bulletin. Better get back on the street, Roger, everyone is out on a call."

After he left the station, Sergeant Breen wrote a memo to Captain Telstra, recommending Hitchcock for a service commendation for saving a citizen's life and taking dangerous drugs off the street.

Hitchcock returned to the Hilltop Inn, hoping to find either the Cadillac or Hatch himself, but neither were there. Now that Sergeant Breen had circulated his reports, the Patrol, Detective and Traffic Divisions would be on the lookout for Tyrone Hatch.

CHAPTER 5

FROM TACOMA WITH LOVE

Wednesday came—Friday for Hitchcock. After a few hours of patrolling and taking calls, his gut instinct told him to visit the bar at the Wagon Wheel. The attractive barmaid who had been making eyes at him before was there. She was in her early twenties, neck-length dark brown hair, fair skin; slim and buxom. She was always friendly and seemed modest and genuine. He knew her name was Gayle; that she was single he assumed from her bare ring finger. It was late. He used the opportunity to help her close up and walked her to her car.

"I'm off for the next couple days," he said.

She looked up at him and smiled. "Me too."

"Could I interest you in dinner, out of town, maybe?"

"You could, maybe."

"Six-thirty tomorrow?"

"Yes. Know where I live?"

"Nope."

"It's just up the hill. Follow me," she said, smiling.

He followed her to her apartment four blocks up the hill and walked her to the door.

"I'll be needing' your phone number," he said with a grin.

Dark eyes looked up into his. "Let me have your pen and that little notepad in your shirt pocket."

She wrote her number on the pad and put it back in his shirt pocket. She smiled again and went inside.

He couldn't explain it even to himself the next morning, but he deliberately took breakfast at Brenner Brothers Bakery instead of the Pancake Corral, followed by a trip to the cleaners, and a workout at the gym. He took his El Camino through the local car wash, shined his shoes, dressed, strapped on his off-duty gun, splashed on a little English Leather cologne and arrived at Gayle's apartment precisely on time. She was dressed modestly in a dark skirt, a white, lacy blouse and leather jacket, perfectly coordinated with her hair and makeup.

He took her to a steakhouse in Bothell, well north of Bellevue, where no one knew them and they could talk privately. Right after they ordered from the menu, Gayle laid her cards on the table.

"I don't know if you know anything about me, but if you don't, I want to be the one to tell you that I'm a former junkie," she said.

Hitchcock shifted in his seat, hoping his shock wasn't obvious. She didn't look anything like a former junkie.

"I'd like to hear about that, if it's all right with you."

"My brother Tony and I were raised by our grandmother in Tacoma after our parents died in a car accident when we were almost teenagers. Tony was two years older than me. He was a good, kind kid until our parents died. After that he changed; always in trouble of some kind. First it was pot, then heroin, and, since we were close, I did what he did. I got addicted and ran with the same crowd with Tony until he died right in front of me from an overdose. It was hard, but I was so scared I quit, cold turkey.

"That was four years ago. I came here to start a new life, and, so you'll know, I've never been arrested. You can check me out, if you haven't already. I won't be offended."

Hitchcock was intrigued by her history and her honesty. "What else? High school? Married?" He asked.

"I was seventeen and getting good grades but I dropped out in my senior year after our grandma died. Tony and I were on our own after that. I've never been married, no kids. I did some modeling for local department and clothing stores, but quit when future work was on condition of other demands. Tacoma is a rough town."

He felt foolish that he hadn't checked her record before asking her out, which even she thought he should do. He would check later, but he felt sure of her truthfulness.

It was his turn to step up to the plate. He briefly described his background, his family, the sudden death of his father, which led to his decision to quit college and enlist.

"Where I work we heard about you making that arrest at Charlie's," she said. "That was scary. I'm sure it had something to do with it being payday that day for nearly every business around. Paydays are always busy for the bars and restaurants here.

"The owner and the manager at the Wagon Wheel don't like you guys checking on them all the time, but after that thing at Charlie's and that big fight you were in downtown, they aren't making critical comments anymore. And you ought to know, they may not want you coming around, but they respect you personally—especially now."

Hitchcock kept fishing. "What about the other bars in Eastgate?"

"There's the lounge at the Hilltop—a lot of drugs go through there; hookers too, from what I hear. Some of the white dealers and pimps drink at the Wagon Wheel once in a while. Blacks go to the Hilltop but avoid our place. Too red-necky for them. The bar owners all know each other, except for the Chinese place near Charlie's."

Hitchcock pretended casual interest. "Oh? You mean The Great Wall? What about it?"

"No one seems to know much. All I hear is that it's a very different crowd there, mostly Orientals from the International District in Seattle. Maybe it's the location, but our customers, if they go anywhere else at all, have a circuit of us, Charlie's and the Steak Out, and once in a while the Blue Dolphin, that little lounge on the other side of the freeway, but I never hear anything about the Chinese place."

"Want to help me do some good?" he asked.

"Sure. What?"

She accepted his offer of modest pay from his own pocket to inform on criminal activity in Eastgate. Hitchcock knew he was on dangerous ground. Gayle was a beauty. He regretted there could be no romance. "The three deadly sins that destroy cops are bucks, broads and booze," Sergeant Baxter told him during his first night on duty, probably out of an educated guess that women were Hitchcock's weakness.

The evening lasted long; the later the hour, the more Gayle divulged tidbits about names, places, inside information that had no meaning to her, but the names she mentioned were familiar to him and opened his eyes about the drugs, hookers and armed men that often stopped by for a drink, a meal, drugs or sex on their way through Eastgate.

By evening's end Hitchcock had a new perspective on his beat, and his first informant. The drive back to Bellevue was quiet. Gayle stood at her door, awaiting a goodnight kiss. He hesitated, but not for long. He was male and single, what could he do? He was surprised at how well she kissed. He kissed her again and wanted more, but stopped. *It isn't supposed to work this way, at least not so soon,* he thought.

That night he committed to paper all he had learned from Gayle and made a copy for Sergeant Breen without naming her. He doubled the ammunition he expended in practice with his service revolver and bought a more powerful pair of binoculars.

On Saturday, he ran statewide and nationwide criminal history checks on Gayle. Just as she said, she was clear of any criminal history, not even a traffic ticket. He verified that her brother Tony died of a heroin overdose; neither Tacoma PD nor the Pierce County Sheriff's Office had any record of Gayle. He verified her identify through her driver's license and Health Department permit. She was legit.

Based on Gayle's revelations about herself, he believed she would be at least as effective as he hoped. Better arrests, identification and interdiction of traffickers, pushers and pimps, burglary rings and stick-up men would result. Paying her for her work would be a hard sell to Sergeant Breen, but he had a feeling it would worth it to pay her from his own pocket if he had to. He looked forward to the coming week.

CHAPTER 6
THE CESSPOOL

The new bar in town was a funky, hard rock kind of place called The Trunk Lid. It was as "un-Bellevue" as it could get. Bellevue watering holes fell into one of two types: staid, white-collar cocktail lounges where men wore suits and ties and the women wore dresses. The other type were the neighborhood taverns, American versions of English pubs; the patrons were younger and more blue-collar. In Old Bellevue they were few and far between.

The Trunk Lid opened in District Four, the industrial zone in the geographic center of the city. By word-of-mouth only, it became an overnight success.

It was located in a concrete, low-ceilinged cavern, a former warehouse with few windows. Even vacant in the daytime it had an ominous aura. The owners were the new breed of entrepreneurs: pseudo-hippy young white dudes sporting afro hairdos and handlebar mustaches, wearing large-collared shirts and bell-bottom jeans; promoters of cocaine and pot as the 'in' thing. Underneath the hip hairdos and clothes, they were greedy opportunists tapping into the latest fad.

They filled the cavern with used chairs and tables, pool tables, a stage, sound system, and deep sofas along the walls. Some of the barmaids and waitresses were rough, crude women and their biker-gang boyfriends, possible ex-convicts, were hired as bouncers. They easily thrilled and intimidated the sheltered upper middle-class Bellevue types who ventured in for a taste of the wild side, as outlaw bikers occasionally rode their Harley's onto the dance floor.

Once the word got out that ID would only be only at, kids in their late teens went there in droves to get drunk, get high and act up like adults.

On the second Friday of November, Mark Forbes had physically and mentally recovered enough from his injuries at the Village Inn fight that he was back on duty. He was assigned District Four, which he liked because he would be working next to Joel Otis in District Seven, whose acceptance he craved. Some of the other officers noticed that Forbes was beginning to emulate Otis, to the point of walking like him and smoking cigars like Otis did.

An hour into his shift, Forbes stopped a car for speeding along the road in front of The Trunk Lid. During the stop, a group of hecklers in the parking lot taunted him with obscenities while on their way into the Lid. He recognized one of the males as an eighteen-year-old he had arrested for disorderly conduct two weeks earlier. Forbes saw making an arrest by himself here as a chance to redeem his reputation after being beaten so easily in the brawl outside the Village Inn.

"Three Zero Four, Radio. I'm clear the traffic stop. I'll be out on a bar-check at The Trunk Lid. Saw a minor I know going inside. Going in to make the arrest."

The dispatcher replied: "Received. Three Zero Four out at The Trunk Lid to make an arrest at 2116 hours. Will you be needing a backup?"

Forbes, the body builder who felt the need to redeem himself in the eyes of his brother officers, replied: "Negative, Radio. I can handle it."

Hard rock music blared all the way to the street through the closed doors. It blasted Forbes in the face when he walked in. The bearded bouncer at the door was a hard-core outlaw biker type. His sleeveless denim vest with the colors of his gang on the back exposed the tattoos on his meaty arms. He glared hatefully at Forbes.

For a fleeting moment, it occurred to Forbes that maybe, just maybe, he should back out and wait for a backup. The thought of the "attaboys" he would get from his peers and his sergeant for single-handedly facing down a crowd of punks overrode his better judgment. Forbes strode into the dark realm of a bar filled with hostile people as if he was a one-man army.

The music that came on as Forbes threaded his way into the crowd was the latest protest song, *"Ohio"* by Crosby Stills, Nash & Young, released after the shooting deaths of four student protestors by Ohio National Guardsmen at Kent State University last spring. The sight of a lone uniformed policeman angered the crowd, whose inhibitions were lowered by alcohol and drug consumption. This, combined with the marching cadence of defiant protest lyrics, the stage was set for what happened next.

Tin soldiers and Nixon's coming
We're finally on our own
This summer I hear the drumming
Four Dead in O-hi-o
Four Dead in O-hi-o

Imagining himself as Dirty Harry in uniform, Forbes angered the crowd further with his swaggering walk and pushing aside even the couples dancing to the music, as his eyes searched for the underage male he saw entering minutes ago. The crowd was quick to turn ugly:

"Better watch who you shove, pig."

"What'cha doin' here, pig?"

"Got no back-up, Jack?"

"Gonna shoot us too? Looking for somebody to club, oinker bastard?"

Forbes ignored the insults and kept looking for Barry, the minor he knew. By now he was deep into the crowd, far from the front door. He could smell marijuana smoke. Then it hit him. He had gone too far in; he was surrounded. Somewhere along the wall a flame flared up. Forbes saw a tall, thin long-haired male sucking on a metal pipe, looking at him daringly. Fear chilled Forbes' limbs. He realized he would have to fight his way out if he made an arrest, but still, this was his chance to redeem himself after being so quickly beaten in the only real fight of his life. How humiliated he felt, lying on the pavement with two other officers, watching Hitchcock and Otis crush Beecham and McMinn so fast they made it look easy.

Forbes' heart was in his throat, but he couldn't back out now. With something just short of a death wish, Forbes moved deeper into the dark recesses. A flame flared up in a far corner to his left. He smelled marijuana smoke and looked toward the wall. A couple was on a couch, puffing on a bong. They looked at him, too stoned to react. He ignored them and continued his search for the minor he was after until he found him in the back, sitting on a sofa with two other friends, drinking beer, staring defiantly, blowing smoke at him as he approached; mocking his presence.

"You're under arrest for minor-in-possession, Barry. Let's go," Forbes ordered.

Barry and his friends were high and drunk; they laughed at Forbes as he stood in front of them. "No way, man. I ain't goin' anywhere with you," Barry said. "You're outnumbered, in case you're too stupid to notice."

Forbes steeled himself and grabbed Barry by the arm and pulled him off the couch. "I said you're under arrest, and resisting arrest will be an additional charge." He put an arm lock on Barry and reached for his handcuffs. Two other youths grabbed Barry and began pulling him away from Forbes. "Get the pig!" someone yelled. Another youth threw a punch at Forbes, hitting him on the shoulder. Someone kicked him in the butt. The song lyrics and the marching drum beat stirred the crowd that was circling Forbes as he struggled to secure his prisoner:

Gotta get down to it
Soldiers are cutting us down
Should have been done long ago
What if you knew her
And found her dead on the ground?
How can you run when you know?
Four dead in O-hi-o
Four dead in O-hi-o

Never had Forbes been so afraid. In his police uniform he was a lone target in a darkened, noisy bar surrounded by an angry, drunken mob, unimpressed with authority. Mild injury was the best he could hope for.

He forcefully shoved his prisoner's friends back and snapped a handcuff on the prisoner's right wrist, pulled him close and said in his ear "We're going out of here together, even if it's by ambulance."

The prisoner shouted to the crowd, "Hey, the pig just threatened me! Get him!" Two young men from the crowd shoved Forbes from behind. Almost paralyzed with fear, Forbes tightened his grip on his prisoner.

The ruckus got the attention of four off-duty Bellevue motorcycle officers in plain clothes on the other side of the bar. Sergeant Bill Harris of the Traffic Division and three of his men happened to stop by after post-shift training for a beer at the new bar before going home. Harris asked a barmaid, "What's going on over there?"

"Some stupid pig picked the wrong place to make an arrest. Looks like he'll get thrown out of here headfirst! You guys oughta go see it," she said, laughing.

"Yeah, we'll do just that," Harris said. The four traffic men threaded their way through the crowd to the hecklers who were about to take Forbes down and free his prisoner. They barged in from behind, pretending to be confused drunks who didn't know whose side to be on, shoving and yelling, "Hey, yeah, let's get 'em!" "C'mon, let's fight!"

In the free-for-all that followed, the mob began fighting each other and Forbes, recognizing his off-duty comrades, clapped the other handcuff on his prisoner and used him as shield and battering ram to force his way through the crowd to his patrol car where he belted him into the back seat. Forbes was hyperventilating as he keyed his mike:

> "Three Zero Four to Radio," he said, his voice raspy, "clearing a disturbance at The Trunk Lid with one in custody." In his haste to leave, Forbes forgot about the four off-duty officers still in the bar, never thinking that they might need help.

"I want my phone call!" Barry shouted at Forbes in the booking room. "My dad will have your job for this!"

Less than an hour later, Barry's father appeared at the front desk. He was in his mid-forties, well-groomed, wearing expensive pleated tan dress slacks, brown Gucci loafers, a red silk shirt, gold Rolex watch, brown leather car-coat. His face was red with indignation and he smelled of alcohol.

"You're holding my son here—bring me the duty sergeant" he ordered the desk clerk.

Sergeant Breen met him. "Your son was arrested for being a minor in possession of alcohol in an adult drinking establishment. The officer recognized your son from a previous arrest, and therefore knew he is a minor. He arrested your son, who with several of his friends not only resisted the arrest, they assaulted the officer and your son attempted to escape custody."

"This is ridiculous!" the father shouted. "Barry is a good boy. We'll get this settled on Monday. I'll sign for Barry. Bring him here."

"There are too many serious charges for that. What's going to happen is that Barry goes to jail until he sees a judge, which will probably be on Monday. Again, he was arrested for four offenses: drinking alcohol in a public bar as a minor, resisting arrest, he and his friends assaulted the officer and he tried to escape. It is possible that your son will be charged with a felony for assaulting a police officer and attempted escape."

The father scoffed at Breen. "Apparently you don't know just who I am, Sergeant. Your Chief and I are good friends. We golf together. As a business owner here, I pay your salary. I can have your badge and the officer's badge for this, just like *that,*" he said, snapping his fingers "Now let my son go. I'll be responsible for him. I don't want him exposed to criminal elements in jail."

"The charges are too many and too serious. He goes downtown and stays there until he sees a judge."

"You'll be hearing from my attorney, Sergeant!" the father shouted.

"You may tell your attorney I am Sergeant Jack Breen. Good night, sir"

The father glared at Breen. "Now I see why the kids call you guys P.I.G. That's what you are!"

Sergeant Breen knew complaints would be filed. He began his own investigation right then. After speaking with Sergeant Harris by phone, he brought Forbes into his office. "Tell me everything that happened there tonight."

After listening to Forbes' account, Breen set him in an empty office to write a detailed report. Then he called Captain Delstra at home.

"Sorry to bother you so late, Erik, but something's come up that you should know about before we get any further into the weekend."

Delstra waited several seconds after Breen finished before answering. "At the very least, Forbes was reckless in not having a backup with him before he entered a crowded tavern to make an arrest," Delstra said.

"Think what would have happened if someone took his gun during the struggle and someone got shot. It also bothers me that Forbes abandoned the four off duty traffic officers who saved him in the bar; he didn't even bother to tell anyone they were there and might need help. What if they were hurt? The fact that no one from the bar tried to help Forbes or even called the station for help is grounds for an investigation that should result in the suspension or revocation of their business and liquor licenses."

After a short pause, Delstra continued. "Starting tomorrow night, bar checks at The Trunk Lid will be done by no less than four officers in helmets. They are to check ID of anyone they suspect of being underage, arrest underage patrons, drug users in the act, identify the bartender for later referral of charges. Do not put Forbes on that team. It would look like revenge if he is one of the officers. Put him downtown and leave him there.

"I want Otis and Hitchcock to head the team, along with two other officers you pick. You know the men on your squad. Pick two more who are *intentional* cops—like Otis and Hitchcock—who are here to be policemen, not to climb the ladder or just do their first year twenty times over for the pay and the benefits. You are free to give them additional instructions as you see fit. Have all reports ready for me on Monday. Keep me informed of anything else that happens, no matter how late it is."

Breen was meditative as he hung up the phone. He understood Delstra's decision was based on his knowledge of the personnel files of Otis and Hitchcock as well as their decisive ending of the parking lot brawl at the Village Inn. They were hometown boys who grew up next door to each other. Both came from stable families and served in combat as Army medics in Vietnam; both had experienced killing.

Otis, Breen knew, was six or seven years older than Hitchcock and had convinced Hitchcock to join Bellevue instead of the Seattle department. Otis's file placed him in Vietnam during the final days of President Eisenhower, when the Viet Cong forces were known as the Viet Minh. The secrecy of his service indicated he may have been on the find-and-kill missions that targeted communist leaders. It was rumored that the skills Otis demonstrated in the baton fight in the Village Inn parking lot he had acquired in Southeast Asia, but no one knew for sure, and no one asked.

Breen also knew from reading Hitchcock's service record that he served two tours of duty in Vietnam, that he was based in Phu Loi the first time. The details of his second tour were undisclosed. Breen was curious about Hitchcock's second tour, but he knew better than to ask.

After Forbes left to take his prisoner to the county jail, Sergeant Breen drove to The Trunk Lid. He parked about forty yards away, shut down his engine and lights, and turned down the volume of his radio. His supervisor's car was a black-and-white without the roof-mounted emergency red light and spotlight, so it would be less noticeable at a distance in the dark. He rolled his window down to listen.

Small groups of long-haired young men, some hanging on their women, staggered outside, heading for their cars. Raucous laughter and cursing was carried by the night air as if they were within feet of him. Some sat in their cars in the dark for long minutes before starting up and leaving. He decided to have LaPerle meet him and do a bar-check there. As he reached for his mike, LaPerle's voice came on the air.

"Three Zero Three, Radio, I am en route to the station with one in custody." LaPerle was his last available unit. The Lid would have to wait until tomorrow.

CHAPTER 7
THE SMACKDOWN

2 p.m. Saturday afternoon.

Hitchcock picked up Gayle at her apartment and headed east on the freeway. She was dressed in a black leather jacket over a pale gray turtleneck cashmere sweater, blue jeans, and clog-style high-heeled shoes that made her look tall. She smelled as fresh and clean as she appeared and her dark hair set off her ivory complexion. Any man would be proud to be seen with her.

"Here's your first case," he said, handing her a folded slip of note paper. "People are dying from this guy's heroin. It's from Vietnam, I'm told. He's wanted in Seattle and we want him on an overdose case and a stolen car here last week."

Gayle read the handwritten information. "Tyrone …" she repeated the name thoughtfully. "This week I heard one of our regulars mention a Tyrone who's been hanging out at the Hilltop a lot. She works there part time."

"How often do you see her?"

"Mostly Friday and Saturday nights. She comes in with her husband and another couple on Fridays after bowling; Saturdays she comes in alone, so she must work then."

"What kind of work does your customer do there?"

"She cleans bedrooms after people leave so they can be rented again."

"You mean by the hour, I suppose,"

"Yes. That's why she works there nights. She told me I would be shocked to see who uses those rooms. Where're we going, by the way?"

"I thought we'd go to Issaquah for a bite before I go to work."

Gayle smiled contentedly. "Sounds good. Remember, I work tonight too."

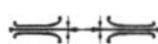

7:45 p.m. Saturday Shift Briefing.

Sergeant Breen stood at the podium. "Listen up. Last night, Mark Forbes was attacked by a crowd at The Trunk Lid when he arrested a minor who was drinking there. If it weren't for the help of Bill Harris and three motor officers who happened to be there off duty, I don't know what would have happened. Per Captain Delstra, there'll be temporary changes in district assignments. For the next week at least, bar-checks at The Trunk Lid will be done by no fewer than four officers at a time, in helmets."

Forbes grinned excitedly. Now he would have his revenge.

Breen continued: "From what I have heard and have seen for myself, drugs are openly being used inside the bar and outside in the parking lot. So here are the changes Captain Delstra wants: the bar-check team will be headed by Otis and Hitchcock, plus Walker and Sherman. Otis and Hitchcock will be a roving two-man unit tonight, Three Zero Nine. Forbes will be in District Three, Sherman will take District Four, and will keep an eye on the size of the crowd coming to The Trunk Lid. Allard in Six, LaPerle in Seven, Walker in Eight. Districts One and Two will keep your normal assignments. Dis-missed!"

Forbes left the squad room seething with anger. Not only were there no pats on the back for bravery as he expected, he was excluded from participating in a return to roust The Trunk Lid with force; his revenge on the bar was denied. It wasn't supposed to be this way. Once again honor and recognition eluded him; he was being punished instead. District Three was about the deadest in the city; a desert full of nice people when it came to criminal activity.

At 10 p.m. Sherman radioed Otis that The Trunk Lid parking lot was full. The four-officer special detail met out of view behind the bar. They readied their gear and put on their helmets. Otis handed out an extra set of handcuffs to each officer and laid out the plan:

> "We go in two abreast, Roger and me first. We stay together. When one stops for any reason, we all stop. Arrest anyone who gives us trouble or won't produce ID or is using dope. When we check the men's room, two go in, two guard outside."

Otis keyed the mike of his portable radio. "Three Zero Nine to Four-Twenty."

"Three Zero Nine go ahead," Sergeant Breen answered.

"We're out on that bar check."

"Received."

Inside the bar, filled with smoke and dim lights, the music of Santana's "*Black Magic Woman*" was playing. The smell of cigarette and marijuana smoke hung in the air. The bouncer at the door was an outlaw biker type--a different one from last night with large tattooed arms. He wore his gang colors on a filthy denim vest, a black bandana, greasy jeans, and heavy black Wellington boots.

He glared and clenched his fists when the team of four marched into the bar, helmeted, two abreast.

The crowd near the door was taken aback. Nervous, even frightened mutterings could be heard along with four-letter expletives. But there were no challenges; the crowd nearest the door parted like water, making way as the helmeted four penetrated deeper into the cavern where more than a dozen couples were dancing.

Otis saw Hitchcock suddenly stop and stare at the dance floor. He understood why when he looked at the crowd there. *She* was there. Hitchcock's old flame, Ruby: blonde, intensely sensual, dramatically voluptuous. Women have plastic surgeries to look like she did. All the men were mesmerized by her as she danced with a wormy-looking, mustached weasel with hair to his shoulders. Seeing her again captivated Hitchcock, and the lyrics fit the moment:

You got your spell on me, baby.
You got your spell on me, baby.
Yes, you got your spell on me, baby,
Turnin' my heart into stone
I need you so bad,
Black Magic Woman I can't leave you alone

For a moment Hitchcock was back in time to a wild love affair with a woman a little older than himself, to an engagement party, and wedding plans that never were. But Ruby didn't see him. A nudge on the elbow and a "we're here on business" look from Otis brought Hitchcock back to reality.

The four-man team moved deeper into the crowd, bold but not pushy, not swaggering but confidently in charge, and the crowd saw it. Hitchcock spotted a long-haired, bearded male standing outside the men's room, as if guarding it, nervously puffing on a cigarette as he watched the officers. Hitchcock nudged Otis. "Restroom!"

The long-hair rushed into the restroom when he saw the officers heading in his direction. Hitchcock and Otis burst through the door into a cloud of marijuana smoke, knocking the "guard" into the wall as they charged in where three men stood; two of them were simultaneously flushing toilets.

They grabbed the three men and threw them against the wall. "Hands on the wall and spread your feet—now!" Otis commanded. He stood guard while Hitchcock searched the men. On two men, he found marijuana pipes and plastic baggies containing what surely was marijuana. The third man had about a half ounce of white powder in a clear plastic baggie in his shirt pocket.

Seizing the baggie, Hitchcock held it up to the man's face. "What's this? Heroin?"

"It's just a little coke, man. I don't do heroin."

"You're all under arrest for possession of a controlled substance," Hitchcock recited their Miranda warning rights as Otis handcuffed them. The shocked crowd muttered nervously but made way for them without a peep of challenge as they marched their prisoners toward the door.

Sherman spotted a kid he knew from a recent shoplifting arrest to be a juvenile. The kid was holding a beer, sitting at a table with two girls and another male; four open bottles of Olympia beer were on the table. Sherman motioned to Otis to wait.

"You're under arrest, Scott, minor in possession. Let's go," Sherman said. The kid shook his head and cursed under his breath as he got up from the table. Sherman cuffed him and handed him to Walker. He looked at the other three; they all looked too young to be there. "Let's see your ID—now," Sherman commanded. Only the other male was twenty-one; the two girls were under age. Borrowing handcuffs from Otis, Sherman arrested both girls.

The officers strode to the front door with six handcuffed prisoners in tow. Unlike the previous night, the mutterings of protest coming from the crowd were few and timid. The bouncer blocked the door as the team approached, glowering and clenching his fists. Walker stepped ahead of Hitchcock and Otis.

"Make way or you'll be going with us." The bouncer refused to step aside. He was taller and heavier than Walker, but to Walker he was more image than substance. Beneath his barbaric exterior he was weakened by a lifestyle of dissipation. Walker brushed him aside with the edge of his forearm as easily as if he were a manikin.

"Do stick around," Walker told the bouncer as he held the door open for the team and their prisoners to go outside.

Walker returned to the bar while his team was frisking their prisoners and radioing for patrol cars for transport. He found the bouncer just inside the door talking to a small crowd.

"You're under arrest for obstructing a public officer," he said. "You can come peaceably or the hard way. Choose the hard way and resisting arrest will be an added charge. Your choice--pick one."

He read in the bouncer's eyes that he would throw a punch with his right, so he reached for the bouncer's arm with his left hand. The punch came. Walker caught the fist by the knuckles in midair with his huge right hand and squeezed. The bouncer tried to jerk his hand away but Walker's grip was too strong. He tried to throw a punch with his left but stopped when pain shot through his arm as Walker continued crushing his right fist. He winced and his knees buckled from the pain as Walker kept squeezing. A cracking sound was heard as the cartilage between the knuckles broke.

The hushed crowd stayed back as Walker kept squeezing and took the biker facedown onto the floor, crying like a baby and begging to be let go as Walker clapped the cuffs on him, and half-dragged him through the doors. The crowd laughed as the biker yelled, "You broke my hand! You broke my - - - hand!" as Walker stuffed him into the back of a patrol car.

While they waited for more units to take their prisoners to the station, Otis returned to the bar with Walker and his citation book. "Let's see your ID, now!" Otis said to the bartender.

"What for?"

"Serving alcohol to minors. Refuse even once, hesitate, and I'll take you to jail and close this place right now and the state liquor board will hear about it."

Otis cited the bartender and returned to his men and prisoners outside.

It took an hour to book all the prisoners and write reports and fill out lab request forms for drug testing. Hitchcock was sitting across a table in the squad room when he turned to Otis as they finished. "I've got a gut feeling we should get back to The Lid," he said.

Otis nodded. "So do I--let's go. You drive."

On their way out of the station parking lot, Otis asked Hitchcock, "Was that who I think it was on the dance floor tonight?"

"Yep."

"Must have been hard to see her in a dump like that; dancing with a guy like she was with. Ruby's changed so much I didn't recognize her at first."

Hitchcock kept his eyes on the road. "The times have changed us. The war has changed us. We've taken different paths—we're different people now. What we once had is gone."

Otis nodded, "Still, I could see it bothered you to see her like that."

"It bothered me."

"These times have changed us all, Kid."

It was 1:14 a.m. when they cruised past The Trunk Lid. Most of the cars were gone. Hitchcock continued up the road until he crested out of sight, then hung a left onto a side street and doubled back. He approached along narrow, two-lane streets past closed industrial shops, and killed the lights when he entered the upper parking lot of a boat repair shop at the north end of The Trunk Lid.

From about thirty yards away and slightly above The Trunk Lid parking lot, they scanned the parked cars with binoculars. Nothing. They waited. In minutes two young men came out of the bar and got into a car parked in front of the building. Two flames flared briefly inside the car, then flickered out, their orange lights faintly illuminating the two men in the front seat.

"Look at that! They're shooting up right now, Joel."

"Let's slip on down there and have a look."

They quietly eased out of their patrol car, bending low as they crept among boats and trailers, down a rocky embankment to the lower lot, and slunk, bent over, among parked cars until they reached their target.

"Take the driver side, I'll get the passenger, get our lights on 'em at the same time," Otis whispered.

Hitchcock reached the rear edge of the driver's door. He and Otis stood up and shone their flashlights into the car at the same time. The male in the driver seat had his left arm bared and extended, palm up, surgical tubing tied above the elbow, his right hand inserting a syringe into his left arm above the elbow.

"Police! You're under arrest!" Hitchcock ripped open the door and jerked the needle out of the shocked suspect's arm.

Otis opened the passenger door at the same instant and shined his flashlight in the other man's face to blind him as he shouted "You're under arrest—hands behind your head!"

He pushed a lighter, needle, spoon and a plastic baggie of white powder from his lap to the floor and pulled the passenger out of the car by the front of his shirt.

Both suspects were handcuffed and searched. The one Hitchcock arrested began fidgeting and rolling his head side to side, shifting his weight from one foot to the other, straining against the cuffs.

"Awww, Officerrrr!" He whined. "You don't know what you've duuhhn! I need my fix! Let me go, pleeease! I'm gonna *die* if you don't! C'mon, I'll do anything, tell you anything you want to know if you let me go."

"Shut up, Howie!" the other man snarled.

A small crowd leaving the bar gathered around. Keeping one hand on his prisoner, Otis faced the crowd. "Keep moving. There's nothing here that concerns any of you. Roger, we'll need our car now."

Hitchcock hustled off and came back with the black-and-white. The crowd had dispersed except for two shaggy-haired young men, hands in their pockets, who were arguing with Otis as he held on to both prisoners. Hitchcock stood between them and Otis.

"These men are our prisoners and you are interfering. Stand back—now," Hitchcock said.

"Hey man, be cool. We just wanna know why---"

"Shut up," Hitchcock demanded. "Stand back or I arrest you both for interfering with a public officer. Move it!"

Hands still in their pockets, both men looked at each other, shrugged, turned and shuffled away without a word, meek as mice. The prisoner called Howie was becoming uncontrollably agitated; crying, itching, hopping from one foot to the other, muttering to himself, and making it harder for Otis to hang onto him and the other prisoner. Howie descended into withdrawal; becoming incoherent, beads of cold sweat on his face, runny nose, babbling and shaking.

Otis checked his pulse. "His heart's gonna explode," Otis said to Hitchcock. "We've got to get him to the ER now!" Otis checked his pupils. They were pinpoints. He removed the cuffs from behind and cuffed his hands in front.

"Rest here, Howie. You'll be all right," Otis told him. "Sit on the back seat of our car, lay down if you want while we get a ride to take you to the hospital." Otis eased Howie onto the back seat and grabbed the radio mike.

"Radio, send a unit Code Two to The Trunk Lid parking lot. We have a male adult going into heroin withdrawal and needs immediate medical attention. We have another in custody for felony drug possession."

Sergeant Breen was on the road when he heard Otis's transmission. He shook his head with pleasure and laughed out loud. "Damn if they didn't go right back out and pop that toilet again when it was least expected! Delstra's gonna love it when he reads this," he said to himself.

Breen keyed his radio mike. "Four Twenty, radio. Get that new ambulance service to The Trunk Lid, Code Two. Three Zero Two, respond to The Trunk Lid to follow the ambulance to the ER and maintain custody of the suspect."

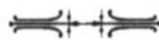

It was past 4 a.m. when Walker entered the squad room where Hitchcock and Otis were finishing their reports, having logged in evidence and booked their prisoner for the morning shift to take to the county jail. "The boys are gettin' together at my place for a few, join us," Walker said.

Hitchcock looked at Otis, who replied, "We'll be there."

CHAPTER 8
THE AFTER HOURS FELLOWSHIP

Hitchcock wondered what he would see when he and Otis arrived at his former digs. By giving his apartment to Walker and prepaying two months' rent, Hitchcock gave a new start to his friend during the final stages of a costly, bitter divorce.

Walker had decorated the place in bachelor-cop style: floor-to-ceiling shelving along one wall of one-by-six planks supported by used bricks. The planks were lined with rows of empty, brown stubby Olympia and Rainier beer bottles—easily over a hundred. A black-and-white 1950s poster of Jack Webb as Sergeant Joe Friday, and another of Marilyn Monroe were thumb-tacked to one wall. Posters of Billy the Kid and Pat Garret adorned the kitchen wall.

His furnishings amounted to a frameless waterbed mattress on the bedroom floor, an old brown leather couch, four beanbag chairs, and a painted "pet rock" on the dilapidated wood coffee table completed the look. A food- encrusted cast iron skillet was on the stove and weights—including dumbbells—were stacked in the dining area.

"Interesting knick-knacks and family photos you got here, Ira," Hitchcock said. "Didn't know you had it in you. Did you get the pet rock from a frizzy-haired hippy girl upstairs--Willow by name---by any chance?"

"Yeah I did. You know her?"

"She gave me a pet rock, too."

"Yeah? And?"

Hitchcock shook his head, smiling. "Nothing else. She's a nice kid—funky, but nice. For a hippy, she sure likes cops. I'd be careful, though."

"Yeah, well in my current position I can't be as choosy as you."

Walker turned to the others and gestured to the array of bottles on the kitchen counter. "Okay boys-- here I got Rainier and Oly, vodka and bourbon and scotch, lime pop and ice, even a few clean glasses. Help yourselves."

Hitchcock looked around the room as he sat down with two fingers of Wild Turkey on ice. "Everybody's here 'cept Forbes. Where's Mark?"

"Pouting and feeling sorry for himself," snorted LaPerle with a shake of his head. "Feels he's been shelved after the scuffle at The Lid."

Otis, being a better judge of men than the others, sank down into a beanbag chair, lit one of his cigars and took a sip of whiskey before he summed it up for everyone.

"Mark's trying to prove himself to us. He can't face the fact that he doesn't know how to fight. What led to his need to prove himself at The Lid was losing the first fight of his life at the Village Inn. He can't get over it."

Allard popped open and chugged half of his fourth bottle of Oly, then out a long belch before chiming in. "Whaddya' mean he can't fight? Mark's real skookum, seen the size of his arms? Works out all th' time."

"Sure. He's a body builder," Otis acknowledged through a cloud of cigar smoke. "But lifting weights in front of a mirror is no substitute for skill, training and experience."

Hitchcock, feeling the warmth of whiskey in his belly, waxed eloquent. “Before this, Mark hadn’t been in a fight in his life. Right? So, he’s emotional about it because he doesn’t know from experience that some you win, some you lose. Wooten got knocked out of the same fight right off, just like Forbes did, but he didn’t let it get him. Lee knows from experience that you can’t win ‘em all. When you lose, you use it as a lesson for the next time.”

“Yup.” Wooten agreed woozily, “nobody likes losing. But fact is, there’s always somebody better or luckier than you. It ain’t the end of the world.”

Sherman, being the first to begin imbibing this morning, by now was properly oiled up. “Mark’s a good guy but he needs to get outta that fru-fru gym, learn to box or go in the Army for a while. Then come back, “he said thickly.

“He can’t—he’s got a wife and a kid. They are why he stayed home when we went. Even though he’s past probation, the brass is watching him and they won’t be happy with the risks he took at the Lid. They’ll see his lack of judgment and actions as a liability and they’ll be wondering what to do with him,” Otis predicted.

“Tonight, Mark handled himself really well at a juvenile party we were sent to,” LaPerle said. “Kids were zonked out on dope, lying on the floor, passed out on furniture, or wherever. Mark arrested the adult, who hosted the party in order to have his pick of doped-up underage girls. Mark actually caught him in the act---an on-view felony arrest.”

Hitchcock spoke up. “One good arrest won’t get him out of the crosshairs of the brass. I’m concerned that they are so worried Mark will do something stupid and costly--trying to prove himself--that they’ll use this latest thing to let him go. Their job is to weigh the risk of keeping him on. He’s got a wife, a kid and another one on the way. To him, losing his first fight and getting in over his head at the Lid *is* the end of the world. Mark needs our help. I propose we all agree to keep an eye on him and help him so he doesn't overreact and get himself killed or fired."

"I agree. Let's all drink to that!" Sherman cheered, now well-oiled up, hoisting his glass in the air.

"Yeah, a toast—to keepin' Forbsh among us!" slurred Allard as he tried to stand up and fell back into his chair, almost dropping his sixth or seventh beer.

"And I propose we all help Allard by not standing up as we drink to Forbes," said LaPerle, to everyone's laughter.

"It's this beanbag chair, not me, Frenchie," Allard said.

"Yeah, right!" LaPerle said in his usual hearty way when he drinks. "We're makin' a pact to help our buddy Forbes, and seal it with a toast," LaPerle announced cheerily.

The sound of glass clinking against glass went around the room as drinks were topped off. When everyone was ready, LaPerle held his glass in the air with all the others and announced, "Here's to our brother Mark Forbes! We all swear to help him stay among us. May he have the presence of mind to listen to us."

As "here-here" was muttered while glasses and bottles were hoisted, Lee Wooten changed the subject.

"Hey, can someone tell me what's with this generation of guys right behind us?" Wooten asked. "When we were their age, we drank, we partied wild, laughed and had fun. None of us even thought about dope. But these kids get together, take pills or shots or whatever, they're on their way out; they're already disconnected, then lay back and zonk out like …" Wooten laid back, spreading his feet and arms outward and his head back, "… that. And the guys I really can't figure out … lot of 'em seem like eunuchs; soft, more interested in dope than girls."

"The latest thing is 'blotter acid,'" Walker said. "Friday night I got a call to a house where the son, seventeen, was scaring the crap out of his parents and his sister. It was LSD that he was on. I arrested him and in his pants pocket, I found three squares of paper that had single dots on them. Took them with me when I took him to the hospital. The doc at Harborview told me the dots are the newest form of LSD sold on the street. It's almost impossible to detect. Put the paper in the mouth, the acid dissolves. It was this kid's third time on acid and he took two that night. Doc told me he'll probably have brain damage."

"The doc is right," Hitchcock said. "LSD causes permanent brain damage. In the middle of the brain is the reticular activating system—or RAS for short. Its function is overall awareness and mental arousal, including sleep levels. It's governed by a fluid the brain makes called serotonin.

"What LSD does is mimic serotonin. When LSD is present, the brain synapses become crowded with too much serotonin-like substance, allowing for impulses to be created and go to the higher levels of the brain, the cerebral cortex, so the person sees things that aren't really there—hallucinations—which the brain interprets as real. People keep doing it for the pleasant effects it can have, but long-term, permanent brain damage is very likely. Already there are cases of people who took it only once who will probably have flashbacks for the rest of their lives when they see a certain color or hear a certain sound."

LaPerle was six-sheets-to-the-wind by now. He looked at Hitchcock in foggy-minded amazement. "How do you know all this?" He asked. "I know you were a medic in the Army, so is that what they taught you?"

"I can answer that," Walker interrupted with a proud big brother grin. "Roger's girlfriend—or I should say *one* of his girlfriends—is a 'doctaahh' at the Overlake ER. A real MD. She makes boo-coo bucks, and she's crazy about Roger."

After the ooohs, ahhhs and attaboys subsided, a grinning Hitchcock said, "Okay, boys, sure, I'm dating Rhonda Kringen. She's been educating me about the drugs we're seeing on the street, and I've been reading up on it also."

LaPerle, always the comedian when he drank, couldn't stop snickering. "Rhonda's been 'educating' you, you say. Hah! I've been to the ER when she's there. She's a *stone fox* with a stethoscope! Easy on the eyes, hard on the heart. I got an idea. - Maybe she could put on a drug education class for us at the station, but on second thought, what if your wives found out? Me? I'm single."

Wooten leaned further back in his beanbag chair, his face slack with scotch, mischief in his grin. "Don't know how I fit in here, boys. You see, I'm not married, but my wife is!" Everyone laughed.

But Hitchcock had fallen into a somber frame of mind. Schoolmates and childhood friends were dying or becoming brain-damaged in the wake of the new drug culture, values were changing drastically and society was becoming more polarized than ever. Finishing his drink, he stood up and put on his jacket. "See you boys Monday night, I'm taking a day of comp time tonight," he said as he left.

Waiting faithfully in the driveway, Jamie wagged his tail joyfully when he saw Hitchcock motoring around the last bend, into view of the cabana.

"Hey, Jamie boy; waitin' for me, eh?" Hitchcock greeted him with a rough rubbing of his hands over his head and neck, which the dog happily leaned into. "I'll rustle up some grub for you, then I got to catch a few winks."

The phone rang as Hitchcock set a metal bowl full of hamburger and dried kibble in front of Jamie.

"Hello?"

"Officer Hitchcock?" an unfamiliar female voice inquired.

"Yes. Who is this?"

"Hi. This is Darlene, from Records. A woman came in here about an hour ago, asking us to leave a message for you to please call her. She left her number. Said her name was Ruby Cain and that you would know her."

Hitchcock's pause was long.

"Officer Hitchcock, are you still there?"

"Yes, sorry. I'm here. Give me the number and then please leave it in my inbox also."

CHAPTER 9
MEETING THE CHATTERTONS

It was nearly 11 a.m. when Hitchcock set his alarm for 6 p.m. and laid down, shoes off, clothes on, Jamie nestled below him on the floor. "Dinner at Mom's at seven," he reminded himself as he stretched out, staring at the ceiling. His body relaxed and consciousness slipped away as he fell into a dream of a past time, of an earth-moving first kiss in a wooded setting by a babbling brook. It was summertime, with a golden-haired girl of rare beauty from the Deep South. She was smiling, whispering, joyously pressing herself hungrily into his embrace; they were new to each other, yet fulfilled, and already as one. Suddenly she began fading. He held her more tightly to keep her from going, and her eyes were locked into his, but she vanished, leaving him empty and alone.

It was a minute before seven when Hitchcock arrived at his mother's tidy, polished brown brick rambler that she bought after her husband's passing. He recognized the cars of his twin sisters in the driveway, but the shiny white Bentley sedan with New York plates he hadn't seen before. He walked up to the front door, fresh flowers in hand, and rang the bell.

His sister Jean opened the door, holding wide her arms. "Happy Thanksgiving, brother of mine, you stranger you!" she hugged him warmly. The aroma of roast turkey and side dishes simmering on the stove reminded him how hungry he was for a home-cooked meal. Taking his jacket, Jean slipped her arm into his and walked him into the kitchen. "Look who's finally come around to see us!" she said to everyone.

Joan, Jean's identical twin, holding her infant son in her arms, gave her brother a hearty one-arm hug. "Happy Thanksgiving, Roger, it's so good to see you. Darren's here too. He's been looking forward to seeing you."

Hitchcock warmly shook hands with his brother-in-law. "Long time, Darren. I see you're taking good care of my sister and increasing the family ranks. Now we've got to find somebody like you for Jean."

"Hey now! Not so fast, you two!" Jean said, laughing.

"Yeah? Well, then, why isn't Matt, your beau, here?" Darren asked.

"You already know the reason, Darren. He wouldn't come because he's scared of Roger."

Darren grinned with approval. "Good! He *ought* to be scared witless of Roger, and Roger should be screening your dates!"

"No way Jose! If he did that I'd be a spinster all my life," Jean said, smiling lovingly at her brother.

Myrna left the stove for a moment to give her son a warm hug. "I'm so glad you came, Roger. Happy Thanksgiving. Let me introduce you to our guests. Roger, please meet Heath Chatterton. Heath, this is my only son, Roger."

A bespectacled, slender man of medium height in his fifties with wavy, slicked-down, graying brown hair parted on the side, a dark mustache and bushy eyebrows---impeccably over-dressed in pleated brown plaid slacks, brown leather suspenders, white dress shirt with cuff links and a red bow tie-- extended his white hand, cold and limp as a dead fish. He so reminded Hitchcock of the old-time cigar-smoking comedian Groucho Marx that he almost laughed.

"I am pleased to meet you, Roger," Chatterton said with a New England accent that was as cold and brittle as his blue eyes. "I have heard so much about you from your mother, and I read in the paper about you too," he said with a tone of Eastern condescension. "I'd like you to meet my wife, Ethel, and my daughter, Emily."

Hitchcock was shocked the second he saw Emily Chatterton. He hadn't expected a matronly girl about his own age, awkwardly put together; tall, flat bosomed with stout hips and legs, long arms, hands almost as big as his, and long flat feet. Dressed in a knee-length pink skirt and a long-sleeved, white silk blouse, her hair was short and mouse brown. She wore horn-rimmed glasses, and looked the part of a rural schoolmarm in a stage play. He smiled politely as he shook her limp-as-a-dead-fish hand, wondering what his mother could be thinking if she thought this was the girl for him.

"So nice to meet you, Roger," Emily said with a shy smile and a lesser trace of New England accent than her parents.

"Ethel, this is Myrna's son, Roger," Chatterton said softly.

Ethel Chatterton was the obvious origin of her daughter's physical characteristics. She was heavy-hipped, with horn-rimmed glasses and short, curly salt-and-pepper hair. She wore a dark gray tweed dress suit, a plain white blouse and high-heeled shoes. "Hello, Roger. Your mother speaks of you often." Her voice was aloof and guarded, her words were crisply accented with short, curled vowels like her husband's.

"Take your seats, everyone! Dinner is ready! Please sit where your name plate is," Myrna ordered.

The table was set with fine white china, sterling silver flatware, softly glowing candles, white tablecloth and linen napkins. The turkey on the china platter had been roasted to a golden brown. The side dishes were arrayed in the center of the table. It was a setting fit for a food magazine.

"Myrna, if it's all right, I would like to say the blessing for us all," Heath Chatterton offered.

"Please do, Heath."

Chatterton cleared his throat as everyone bowed their heads. "Lord, we thank thee for this thy bounty, and forgive us all for the wrongs we do, especially this immoral war. Amen."

An uneasy silence cloaked the table. Myrna fidgeted in her chair. Jean, Joan and Darren looked uneasily at Roger, who ignored the bait. "Pass the turkey and gravy, Darren, I haven't eaten like this in a long time," Hitchcock said.

Heath Chatterton wasted no time. "So, Roger, I would like you to know that although we haven't met until now, we do have something in common. I bet you can't guess what that is," he said as he helped himself to the dishes and passed them along.

"You are right, Heath, I have no clue as what we have in common. What is it?"

A smug smile came across Chatterton's face. "We are close friends with someone at your department you certainly must know. He's a rising star there, soon to be chief. I'll bet you didn't know that."

"No," Hitchcock said, as he took large slice of turkey onto his plate, drenched it with gravy and took his first bite. "I didn't know that. Who would that be?"

Chatterton seemed genuinely shocked. "Why, the man who runs the whole show there, of course—Rowland Bostwick. *Lieutenant* Bostwick, to *you*, of course. You may not know it, but his family is from The Hamptons, just as we are. His family came over from England before the War of Independence, just as ours did. Your department was a mess before Rowlie came along. He's been cleaning up the drugs and violent crime in Bellevue, making arrests and directing the men on how they should do their duty, and they all look up to him. Because he's a family friend, I get to hear all the inside scoop, confidentially, of course. I probably know more about your department than you do," Chatterton said, smiling smugly.

Hitchcock at first thought Chatterton was joking, He choked on his food trying to stifle an outburst of laughter when he realized Chatterton might be serious. Myrna leaned across the table in concern. "Quick, Darren! Slap him on the back. Are you all right, Roger?"

Clearing his throat as Darren thumped his back, Hitchcock turned away to cough and get the smile off his face. *Is this guy a comedian?* he wondered. *If so, he's good.* "I'm fine, Mom; thanks, Darren."

Doing his best to stifle his laughter, Hitchcock asked Chatterton, "So Bostwick tells you these things, does he?"

Heath Chatterton smiled broadly. "Yes, and again, it's *Lieutenant* Bostwick to you, but *Rowlie* to us; he is one of us, a fine man. He'll be the next chief, right after Sean Carter retires. He says it's a sure thing, thanks mostly to the City Manager, whose wife is also from The Hamptons. Rowlie's meeting with the City Manager quite a bit these days. Says he'll make a lot of changes in the department, clean it up right away."

Hitchcock struggled mightily to conceal his shock and amusement. "He does, does he? What 'cleaning up' would he do—did he tell you?"

"Yes, as a matter of fact," Chatterton said, his face beaming with his own self-importance. "Now, no offense, Roger, but Rowlie thinks the department shouldn't hire war veterans. Too dangerous. And I am not the only one in the city who agrees with him. Men who have been in combat are damaged goods, so to speak; liable to go on a rampage at any time. It's a pity, but we should keep them at a safe distance from the rest of us. Rowlie says he'll flush out the war veterans and hire only non-military people. Also, officers will be uniformed in slacks, white shirts and neckties, with blue sport coats instead of those military-looking uniforms. He'll also disarm the officers; they'll only carry non-lethal things like clubs and sprays. Guns will be held in the station, released only when there is an emergency. That's how the Brits do it, and it works well for them."

"Except this is America, not Britain."

"Ah, yes," Chatterton continued in a sing-song lilt as he sawed off another hunk of turkey for himself, "but by disarming the police first," he said, pointing one finger in the air like a brown-nosing kid in elementary school, "we set a precedent that will be returned. The basic good that is in every man will respond in kind, except for a few exceptions, and all this violence will drop sharply."

Hitchcock could hardly believe his ears. *Is this guy putting me on?* he asked himself.

He considered explaining to Chatterton that officers are protected from arbitrary firing by the Civil Service Commission, and that the rate of officers killed on duty is up sharply since the late 60s, but he decided to learn more by holding his silence and letting him talk. As he expected, Chatterton kept chattering as he ate.

"So, Roger, I read in the paper about your beating up that poor fellow a few weeks ago, and the later article about your boxing career. How was it?"

"How was what?"

"Sorry. I was referring to boxing."

"It was great. I learned a lot about life from it. Hard work, discipline, persevering when the outlook is bad. My Dad boxed semi-professionally before and after the war. He paid his way through medical school with the prize money he won. He taught me himself at first, and later I trained weekly at the club in Seattle where dad trained and also at home with a coach who was a friend of Dad's almost every day after school. I boxed competitively for nine years."

Chatterton wasn't smiling or looking at Hitchcock now. "I see," he said as he stared at his plate. "Wouldn't it have been better to play a team sport?"

Hitchcock smiled coolly. "I did, Heath. I played junior varsity and varsity baseball every spring. I cut back on ring training to play ball."

"That was in high school? Sammamish High?"

"Yes. I'm surprised you know about it."

"Oh yes," Chatterton said in a solemn tone, shaking his head. "Rowlie tells me that all the criminals and all the ones who became policemen who grew up in Bellevue were from Sammamish High School."

Everyone at the dinner table was shocked and angry, but Hitchcock changed the subject.

"As for 'beating up' the man in the Village Inn parking lot, as you put it, Heath," Hitchcock said, ignoring Chatterton's attack. "I used only enough force to stop him. It was as the paper said, Beecham and his partner had already beaten four people to the pavement, one was a woman and three were officers. Beecham was still beating and kicking a fallen officer when I arrived. He tried to do the same to me, but I prevailed. There's nothing more to it than that."

His sister Jean cut in. "I think what you and Joel did was heroic, Roger, you both prevented further injury and saved lives."

"Oh yes, Otis, the other officer," Chatterton said, sneeringly. "We mustn't leave him out of our discussion. Myrna tells me his family lived next door to you when you were growing up. That he is older than you and an influence on you."

Hitchcock nodded. "Yes. Joel is older than me. Like an older brother. He taught me to play baseball when we were kids..."

But Chatterton wasn't listening, he was thinking ahead to his next probing. "You were in Vietnam. What do you think of the war?"

Myrna nervously interjected. "Excuse me, Heath, but this is Thanksgiving. Shouldn't we change to more pleasant subjects?"

"It's alright, Mom, I will answer Heath's question." Looking at Chatterton, Hitchcock said, "I agree with the war, Heath. I've been there twice, and I wasn't drafted, I volunteered for a three-year hitch. I've seen what kind of people the communists are. They are cruel and skilled at wearing their enemies down in every way possible, psychologically as well as militarily. To them the ends justifies the means. Communism has been spreading since the end of the war. It's better to fight its spread over there than here. The biggest threat to our winning is the news media and weak politicians, not the communist forces in Asia. We've won every time on the battlefield, but we're losing it here at home and that's what the communists are counting on."

"I agree with you, Roger," Darren said in support. "If I hadn't found Joan, I'd still be in uniform today."

Chatterton wouldn't let the matter rest. "Whether you know it or not, Roger, the world is changing. The progression toward unionism will lead to socialism and later to a modified form of communism, a world in which the gospel principals of equality and share-and-share-alike are enforced by a benevolent government, and a ruling class, supported by media. It will be a *social* gospel, though, not the one in the Bible, it will guarantee equality for everyone. As this happens, wasteful wars will go away over time and poverty will be a thing of the past. It's the future," he said, smiling smugly.

"You obviously think so but the numbers say you're wrong."

Chatterton's look and smile returned to his natural cold condescension. "I am a pragmatic man, Roger. *Of course* I believe in the factuality of numbers. Proceed, please," he said in a low mocking voice.

"It's simple math, Heath. Take the so-called antiwar movement. The estimated total of participants is in the thousands, wouldn't you say?"

"Most surely. Tens of thousands," Chatterton agreed, cheerfully now.

"And our present military establishment, most of whom are not there as a career, but only for two to four years, is just under four million at any one time," Hitchcock continued. "Those four-plus million volunteers and draftees are perpetually rotating in and out, the ranks are constantly refilled with new people on a monthly basis, all or nearly all of whom support the war or they wouldn't be there. The protestors' numbers are miniscule compared to the numbers of my generation who quietly serve and go back home to build families and careers. The *real* reason the protestors seem so dominant is due to news media bias and Hollywood sensationalism – and those who exploit the turmoil to meet a hidden agenda, such as yours."

Chatterton's smile went away and he blushed red with anger and embarrassment. He had been defeated in argument by a youth. He stopped eating and was silent for long seconds. He needed time to think of something to say to recover.

"Excellent point, Roger!" said Joan, clapping.

"Never thought of it that way, but that's right," Darren added.

Even Ethel Chatterton, the wife, was nodding in silent agreement, looking down, lips pursed.

"Okay, so it is," Chatterton finally conceded. "But there are many of us in positions of influence who want America to lose this war and we are working toward it; secretly, of course. It's time America got a comeuppance. We are working behind the scenes to shape public opinion in that direction, away from our past. What do you think of that?"

Hitchcock looked calmly at Chatterton. "It's not what I think—it's what it is. Those who do that are aiding the enemy. It's called treason, Heath."

He glanced at Ethel. She was silent, looking down, hands in her lap, food barely touched. He looked at Emily—tears filled her eyes. She had looked forward to meeting Roger, but now, thanks to her father, the evening hadn't gone at all as she had hoped, and Hitchcock felt empathy for her.

Like switching television channels, Hitchcock amiably visited with the others on other topics for the rest of the dinner and afterward. He included Emily and Ethel but Heath Chatterton withdrew into a sullen silence. At the end of another hour, Hitchcock kissed his mother and his sisters goodbye, shook hands with Darren and the Chattertons. He could tell Myrna was boiling mad. He looked at Emily. She had been quiet throughout the meal, and barely ate. Tears of hurt and embarrassment filled her eyes as he headed out the door for home. Darren followed him.

"Your mom is so upset with Heath, Roger, she's about to explode. I can't remember ever seeing her so mad. I think I'll ask Chatterton as he leaves how he enjoyed his first and last dinner with the Hitchcocks. Whaddya think?"

Hitchcock laughed and playfully slapped Darren on the shoulder. "Nah, let it go. I purposely gave him enough rope to hang himself with Mom and he did. Besides, I like a good laugh, and Heath gave me plenty to laugh about. If he doesn't know what a fool he made of himself, from the look of it, his wife is sure to inform him on their way home. I hope he isn't as serious about communism and treason as he let on tonight. See ya, Darren."

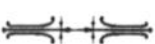

It was cold and raining as he drove back to his digs; a perfect night to build a fire, sit back with a hot drink and relax. He toweled and fed Jamie, and reheated the morning's coffee. The fir logs crackled and poured forth dry heat. He put his feet up by the fire, cup in hand. The rain pattered on the roof, and he smiled as he pondered his conversation with Heath Chatterton, whose strong communist sympathies were a surprise to everyone. Everyone, that is, except perhaps Chatterton's wife and daughter. He wondered if Chatterton's convictions went deep enough to actively support subversive groups, or if he was all talk.

He laughed out loud each time he remembered what Chatterton said about Bostwick "cracking down on crime" and "leading the men," and his plans to "clean up" the department.

His thoughts turned to Ruby. He threw another log on the fire and added whiskey to his coffee. *I've come a long way since it ended, so why should I return her call? What could she possibly want? Seeing her for those few seconds, I realize I'm still not over losing her. Maybe I never will be, maybe it isn't over for her either,* he thought.

The fire had dimmed to glowing embers. Past romantic scenes of himself and Ruby came back and lingered in his mind. He relived their first date, their first intimate time. Eventually he doused the fire with the last of his coffee, kicked his shoes off and stretched out on his bed, still dressed, and slept, dreamlessly this time.

CHAPTER 10
RUBY

Monday, 9 a.m.

The racket of heavy rain on the roof and his dog's cold nose against his face woke him up. He glanced at his clock. Ten hours' sleep straight through. He felt rested and clear-headed. He let Jamie out, refilled his percolator with extra scoops to wake him up enough to think. He let Jamie in, refilled his food bowl and showered. He toweled off, slipped into a clean pair of jeans, and drank his coffee, bitter and black. Fully awake, he dialed Ruby's number, a number he would always remember. A voice he would recognize anywhere answered on the second ring.

"Hello?" she said.

"Good morning, Ruby, it's Roger."

"Yes, I recognize your voice. Hello, Roger." She said matter-of-factly. He listened for a trace of emotion in her voice as she spoke. "After I saw you in the bar Saturday night I thought we could see each other and just talk a bit."

Maybe there's something here after all, he thought. "Sure. When?"

"How about today? I'm not working today so one o'clock would be a good time for me."

"Okay. Where?"

"Remember the Hotel Café in Redmond? It'll be quiet there after the lunch crowd leaves."

"See you there." A strange sense of hope and longing rose within him as he hung up.

The heavy rainfall had stopped by the time Hitchcock left. For good luck he took Jamie with him on the thirty-minute drive. His heart was in his throat as he drove. Redmond was Ruby's home town. He used to think it suited her: beautiful and possessing a certain rural innocence, simple-hearted and focused. After what he saw of her in the bar Saturday night, he knew she had changed. He expected she would test him by telling him things he didn't want to hear. In his heart he had already let her go, and moved on, but only because he had to. Now, to his surprise, with this open door, he found himself hoping against hope…

The Hotel Café was a two-story brick building that was built for loggers and travelers in the early 1900s. The guest rooms on the second floor were no longer rented. Hitchcock never knew what purpose the rooms served now. The ground-floor café was open 24-7. It smelled of fries, ketchup and hamburgers when he walked in. The lunch counter facing the kitchen was empty but several tables and booths along the walls were occupied. For privacy he picked a booth on the far side of the black-and-white checkerboard linoleum floor. The waitress brought two coffees. It wasn't a long wait.

Ruby dominated the room the second she came through the door. She always did. All eyes turned and stared. Blue jeans and a tight black sweater that accentuated her ample bosom and dramatic figure. Her genuinely golden mane overflowed her shoulders, and blue-green eyes deeply set in chiseled features swept the room until they found and locked on Hitchcock as she crossed the room. Old memories of lost love flooded both their minds with every step she took. He got to his feet as she approached and waited for her to sit down.

"Thanks for getting up. The men around here, if they can be called that, don't have manners anymore," she said with a trace of Southern accent as she slid onto the seat.

She gazed at him with a sense of wonder. "I had never seen you in your police uniform before. I didn't recognize you at first because of your helmet, but your build and the way you move, I'd know anywhere. You looked very handsome, and it was very impressive the way you guys took prisoners out of there. Was that Joel, your former neighbor, I saw with you?"

He nodded. "Yes, it was. He convinced me to join Bellevue instead of Seattle when I got out."

"I thought I recognized him," she said, tossing her golden hair back. "You guys were clearly nobody to mess with that night—you had all the 'little boys' there so scared some probably peed their pants, especially when the bouncer everybody was so afraid of lost his hand. That was something from a movie scene," she said with a laugh.

"What's your connection to that place?"

"I've been dating the two greedy slobs who own it. They really think they're cool—they hate the law and serve anybody and everybody who comes in, as you know. And they don't care what else goes on, no matter how illegal it is. The place is wide open, whatever you can think of goes on there. You probably already know that the owners and the customers say bad things about cops, Bellevue cops especially, but after last Saturday there's been a change in attitude. But---"

"But what?"

"But they won't stop what they're doing."

"Which is what?"

"They're up to no good. What they allow in there is just a hint of what goes on. We'll leave it at that."

His heart sank at the thought of her associating with criminals, but said nothing.

She looked him over appreciatively. "You look really good, Roger, I must say. You're obviously taking care of yourself. Women young and old must be fighting over you. The one who lands you will be lucky. So—did you ever return to boxing? You were one of the top candidates in Seattle for turning pro after the Olympics, before your dad passed away."

He shook his head, drinking her in with his eyes. "Not enough time for it now. I train just enough to keep in shape."

"Let me guess—still doing a hundred pushups at a whack like your dad taught you, right?"

He nodded with a grin, pleased that at least she remembered some small details about him. Her presence pleased him. The fiery passion they once knew was barely glowing embers but it was still there. He set aside his distaste for her choice of men and wondered if---

"How come you were in a place like that? A rat-hole joint like that was beneath you just four years ago," he asked.

"Four years ago, we had plans for marriage and family. I loved you—maybe I still do. But we've both changed, Roger. And you know *why* I changed."

He didn't show it, but Hitchcock became unraveled. For him at this moment, there wasn't another woman on the planet who could satisfy his desires and manly lusts. All his progress in recovering from losing her was undone; he wanted her back, he would fight to get her back if the spark that was left was enough. Inwardly he was looking for a thread of hope that it was enough to rebuild on, a chance to start over. He was ready to begin blowing on the remaining embers, to bring them back to life.

There was a pause between them. He looked carefully at Ruby. She wasn't the sweet innocent girl who had been his fiancée, the transplant from Mississippi. That girl was gone. Everything about her now announced her as a loose woman, the kind that turns men unto boys and boys into men.

"Daddy says to tell you 'hello' for him, by the way," she said, ending the awkward silence. "He never approved of you having darkies for friends, but he admired you for excelling against them in boxing. He was pleased when I told him you're a police officer now, like he was back in Mississippi."

Hitchcock grinned. "Say 'hello' to your father for me too. I remember he told me he took a lot of heat for being the first man in his family who didn't belong to the Klan, so I guess he would be upset over the color of some of my friends."

"You and Daddy always got along so well. You were his pick for me."

Was this the opening he needed? "Tell him the .38 he gave me and taught me to shoot I took with me over there. Tell him I carried it with me every day and put it to good use several times. Tell him it saved my life and I still have it."

"I will. He'll be pleased to know that."

They paused again until he broke the silence this time.

"Your 'Dear John' letter to me when I was over there almost got me killed," he said. "But this is now. What about us now, Ruby? I still love you. I don't need to think about it. Don't you miss what we had? Was what happened between us so bad that we can't pick up the pieces and start again where we left off?"

She shook her head slowly, with her eyes locked on his. "No. That part of me is dead because of what happened. Think about it, Roger. Twin boys—*ours*. You were my first man, you would have been my only man, but you abandoned me, you went off to war when you didn't have to, when I needed you. I loved your dad—he was a wonderful man—but for me to be by myself with a baby while you were away in the Army, being around your mom and her disapproval of me, would have been too much. I wanted to have a family with you, settle down, help you through medical school, even if we had to be poor for a while; but no, you had to go fight communists.

"You changed overnight when your father died. The war was heating up, you and your friends were hot-to-trot to get over there to fight. You left me defenseless against your mother's schemes after the abortion. You didn't marry me and take care of me when you had the chance. Your rejection changed me into what I am now. I never thought I would, but I *like* what I am now, Roger,"

"And what are you now, Ruby?" he asked, regretting the question and dreading her answer.

She paused, as if she didn't want to say. "I'm the opposite of you. I smoke pot, Roger. I think it should be legalized. I like cocaine, and I think it should be legalized. I go to the peace demonstrations and I date different men, lots of them. I don't want marriage and I don't want kids—that's all outdated anyway. The whole country's changing except you, Roger. You think the Watts riots were something? You think the war protests are something? The next wave of protest will be bigger: brown people—Mexicans, Indians, and Asians—and women too ... it's not just blacks anymore that will be demonstrating against the Establishment. The old order is going away."

Hitchcock felt heartsick. He expected she would have involvements with other men, but he hadn't expected such a bitter turn to drugs, promiscuity and protest politics. There could be no going back. He was a police officer, a lawman; being with her--a druggie and a political radical--would jeopardize his career. Ruby had crossed the line while he away. It couldn't be, ever again.

"For whatever it's worth, Ruby, I didn't reject you. You knew that, abortion or not, I would have married you. Yes, I should have married you then. I was wrong. If I could do it over again, I'd still have joined the Army, but I would have married you first, had our kids and by this time I'd be out, we'd be parents, raising a family in our own home. The abortion was wrong—we both know it now. But, be honest, no one forced you; it was your responsibility as much as mine. Even so, I will ask you now … will you forgive me?"

Bitter eyes looked deep into him. "Yeah, why not. Won't change anything."

"So why then did you want to see me?"

She shrugged. "When I saw you Saturday night, I felt something. I felt it again when I first got here. But what I am now is where I'm at."

He stood up and reached into his jeans pocket. "How much is a cup here?"

"Just went up to two bits, I guess."

Leaving a buck on the table, he walked her to her car. "I've tried once more to get you back and struck out," he said. "That's two times at bat. Let's let it go at that." She made no reply.

A kaleidoscope of thoughts, emotions and memories dominated his drive back. He and Ruby were different people now. They had irreversibly taken incompatible life paths. Oddly, he felt a sense of release came to him, a satisfaction in knowing that he had done what he could to right his wrongs as best he could and win her back if possible. It wasn't enough. *Some things just aren't meant to be,* he realized. He could finally let go; he could move forward. As for marriage or even love without marriage, there was still a wall of emotional numbness around him that he couldn't control; it was just there. Police work was his only steady passion now.

He still liked the idea of loving again and building a family, but after seeing Ruby today he had learned an important truth: relationships are like eggs; their parts are fragile, and you can't unscramble eggs.

CHAPTER 11

CALM BEFORE THE STORM

At the same time that Hitchcock was returning Ruby's phone call, Captain Erik Delstra arrived at the station to find a tall stack of reports from the weekend on his desk. Among them was a thick, sealed manila envelope marked "confidential." He picked up his phone and dialed 12 for Marjorie, his administrative assistant. "Hold all calls unless it's the Chief. I've got a lot of reading to do."

He read officers' reports on arrests and events at The Trunk Lid. He chuckled with satisfaction when he read of Walker's breaking the hand of the bouncer who tried to punch him, and Otis and Hitchcock's surprise return there and catching two heroin users in the act of shooting up in the parking lot. He made a note to contact the state Liquor Control Board and the City business licensing department to demand the suspension or revocation of the Trunk Lid's liquor and business licenses.

After reading Forbes's report on his Friday night arrest at The Trunk Lid, and the reports of the off-duty officers who saved him from the crowd, Delstra was disturbed. When he coupled what he read with the comments of other Patrol commanders regarding Forbes's growing pattern of aggressiveness toward arrestees, Delstra decided an informal investigation was in order.

The next item was a memo from Sergeant Breen, recommending a service commendation for Hitchcock for saving the life of a local drug addict who was clinically dead when he arrived. Hitchcock revived him and took him to the hospital, barely saving the man's life.

Attached to Breen's report was a letter from the addict's mother, Barbara Fowler; hand delivered. She expressed her thanks to the department for Officer Hitchcock saving her son, whom she affirmed was dead when Hitchcock arrived at her home.

Delstra opened the sealed manila envelope next. In it was a handwritten note from Sergeant Breen addressed to him:

> *"Erik, by pure chance I happened to find this memo lying open on the duty lieutenant's desk. Since not only is the text alarming, but also a violation of the chain of command, I took the liberty of copying it and am submitting the copy to you. I returned the original to Lt. Bostwick. He does not know you have a copy. Jack"*

He felt his blood boil when he read the memo. It was marked '*confidential*' from Bostwick to one of the young intern assistants from the University. Bostwick described his meeting with Officer Hitchcock, in which he accused the officer of "gross insubordination" and "exhibiting strong indications of antisocial behavior with homicidal tendencies stemming from his military service in Vietnam, where he was engaged in killing." Bostwick stated his belief that the department's policy of giving hiring preference to veterans like Hitchcock, is "a troubling mistake" which he will correct when he becomes the department's next chief. Bostwick ended his letter stating he would continue to take steps to ensure Hitchcock's eventual termination.

So, we have our own Benedict Arnold, Delstra thought. He was fuming and needed time to cool down. He had long been suspicious of Bostwick. He was a poor fit in the department who mysteriously kept himself apart from everyone else. His intentions and loyalties were never clear. Delstra resolved to uncover the conspiracy Bostwick was part of and act accordingly.

There was yet another envelope from Sergeant Breen on his desk. In it were two memos. One was from Hitchcock, to Sergeant Breen, reporting that the mother of the heroin addict whose life Hitchcock had saved, named Tyrone Hatch as the source of the heroin. Hitchcock's memo further stated that the Seattle Police know Hatch as a heroin dealer, a pimp and a convicted felon, and named two people who died in Bellevue from overdose on heroin they received from Hatch in the last week.

The other memo was also from Breen, stating the felony warrants for Hatch had been confirmed, adding that Hatch was known to be armed, and to turn women into addicts to become prostitutes for him. Breen had briefed the entire patrol, traffic and detective divisions and posted Hatch's mug shot in the squad room.

Delstra leaned back in his chair, pondering what he just read. What officers are facing now is a different ballgame that what his generation faced on the street just six years ago. Big city crime was spreading into the suburbs now, taking advantage of a naïve, unaware populace. FBI statistics stated that drugs and dealers, prostitutes and pimps, armed robberies, and attacks on officers were increasing in the suburbs, yet city leaders in suburban areas across the country seemed unwilling to acknowledge the facts, that some of the grisliest crimes are starting to happen in the suburbs. Perhaps they just don't know what to do, so they keep their heads in the sand.

More than that, Delstra recognized a significant safety risk his officers faced that Seattle cops didn't---the mind-numbing boredom of routine patrol in quiet suburbs and small towns where nothing happens, day after day, leads to a deadly '*nothing ever happens here*' mindset. Officers in suburbs typically don't get enough intense activity on a consistent basis to develop the dominance and the survival edge they need to win when the chips are down. It was hardly noticed by policy makers that in the last two years, over half of the homicides of police officers have been in suburban departments and rural sheriff's jurisdictions.

Delstra considered that Bellevue is not experiencing a crime wave, per se, but an upsurge in crime that is due in part to the recent massive annexations, and to a lesser extent the current spike in violent crime across the country. Serious matters were happening not only on the streets, but within the Department. In the wake of explosive growth and expansion, the Department's small--town, family atmosphere of the past has been shouldered aside by new competing political factions. What troubled Delstra most was the reluctance by most of the brass to acknowledge the need to modernize operations.

It's as if city leaders are sleepwalking. What will it take for them to wake up and take action? Delstra wondered. He could not have known that within a matter of hours, that wake-up call would arrive.

CHAPTER 12

THE WORK OF THE NEW MATA HARI

Monday, 7:45 p.m.

Two messages were in Hitchcock's inbox when he came in. One was Ruby's phone number, which he tore up, because he had met her already. The other was marked urgent. "Call Mata Hari at 746-xxxx at nine sharp." Mata Hari was a famous woman spy during World War I. She was executed by firing squad when it was learned she was a double agent. Why Hitchcock gave Gayle that code name was unknown to even him, but he recognized the phone number was the Wagon Wheel bar manager's office.

Monday nights are usually quiet. Hitchcock hoped it would stay that way as he rolled out of the station parking lot. There were no calls holding, so he headed straight for the Fowler residence, arriving in minutes.

"Hi, Mrs. Fowler. May I come in to see how Randy is doing?"

"So good of you to stop by, Roger," Barbara said. "It means a lot to us. Randy's doing fine, and he's in his room. Jim, my youngest, says 'thank you' and could he see you some time."

"I'd like to see Jim. Is he home?"

"He's at church now, youth group, but he'll be back later tonight."

"I' dropped by to check on Randy, if I could. May I come in?"

"You know the way," Barbara said, smiling.

He threaded his way through the messy living room, down the hall and knocked at Randy's door. Randy was sitting up in bed, rail-thin and sickly but alive.

"Roger!" he exclaimed. "I didn't expect to see you so soon. You saved my life, man! I'll never be able to repay you for that."

He sat on the edge of the bed. "Glad you made it, Randy. You had a very close call. I hope you never go back now that you're clean. I hate losing friends."

"I'm getting on a good program, by order of the court. Mom worked a deal with the prosecutor today to get me out--patient treatment, meetings with a counselor, all that. If I complete the programs and stay clean for a year, the charge stays off my record. I plan on going to church with Mom and Jim, too. I still might get that job at Lake Hills Chevron; if I do I can walk to work. All this, thanks to you, buddy."

Hitchcock checked his watch. "Sorry to cut this short, Randy, but I got an appointment in fifteen minutes, so I must go now. I'll drop by again soon."

Randy smiled warmly in appreciation of the childhood friend who had saved his life. He extended his hand to Hitchcock. "Got some far-out cop stuff to do, huh? Take care, Roger."

Hitchcock shook hands with him. "I'll see you in a couple days, Randy. Take care."

He went to the nearest public pay phone and called the number he was given. Gayle answered on the first ring.

"Hi Gayle. It's me, Roger. Whatcha got?"

"Hey Roger, I got new info on Tyrone Hatch for you. My girlfriend's still workin' at the Hilltop. She told me today Tyrone Hatch is in and out of there all the time now, hangs out at the bar. He's got a fat white girl with him most of the time, bleach blonde, name's Mae. She drives him around, dominates the other girls Tyrone brings to the motel—she even beats them to make sure they do as he says—Mae does everything for him. Two cars; mostly it's an older white Lincoln, a big boat with fancy wheels, and today, a green Ford Maverick. Hatch carries a revolver; showed it to one of the other cleaning maids yesterday, a young colored girl, as his way of impressing her. She says he told her he's going to kill a white cop with it."

"So where is he now, Gayle? Does your friend know that?"

"Nope, 'cept that he's got two places; one in the Seattle Central District, the other is a house somewhere in Eastgate, somewhere on the south side of the freeway, and close. Because the Seattle cops are looking for him right now, he's almost always in Eastgate."

"A house!" he said in surprise. "Anything else? Like when does he go to the Hilltop? Where else does he go in Bellevue? What time today did she see him in the green Maverick?"

"Don't have that now, Roger. Sorry. I'm working to get more for you as soon as I can."

"Okay. Time is of the essence. You already have my number. I'm giving you our emergency number to call in case you learn where he is, and tell them to call me so I can call you. Are you working tonight?"

"I'm at work until closing at two. I'm going straight home then."

He wasted no time writing up Gayle's information on a standard report form and taking it to Sergeant Breen at the station. Breen read it carefully while Hitchcock waited.

"How did you get this?" Breen asked.

"My female informant, I told you about her."

Breen shook his head in dismay, "Can't believe this is happening in Bellevue, but it is. I've got to alert the rest of the squad right away. For God's sake, keep me posted and be careful, Roger."

"I have no doubt her information is correct. I trust her."

He returned to District Six, nervously keeping on the move, checking and re-checking parking lots and bars. At the same time, Sergeant Breen personally met with each of his officers to ensure they got the information off the air, in case Hatch had a police scanner. He told each of them that Hatch was armed with a revolver and had told someone that he intends to kill a white police officer. He advised Dispatch personnel and advised Captain Delstra by phone.

Still feeling edgy, Hitchcock kept pressing the butt of his service revolver with his elbow as he checked the Wagon Wheel to see for himself that Gayle was there. "Nothing new yet," she mumbled under her breath as she passed him on her way to a table with a tray of drinks.

He checked the parking lot of the Hilltop. Neither the white Cadillac nor the green Maverick were there. He ran the plate of every car or truck there for warrants--no hits. The lounge had few customers.

Like the Hilltop, the Steakout was quiet. The employees outnumbered the customers. He didn't notice the two men who walked out the second he entered. When he returned to his cruiser, the driver door window was smashed out; an act of malice, he assumed. He turned in his car at the city gas pumps, where the shop is. Sherman picked him up.

"Looks like we're a two-man unit for the rest of the shift, Roger" Sherman said with a grin.

"Yeah, it's been so quiet it gives me the creeps, like something's gonna happen," Hitchcock said as he placed the shotgun from his car and his briefcase in the trunk of Sherman's cruiser.

"Yeah? Is this your gut instinct again?" Sherman asked, smiling but only half- joking.

"Probably--maybe. It just feels like something's gonna happen."

Sherman laughed. He was one of the handsomest men on the department; tall and lean like Hitchcock, but on a lighter frame, built like a gymnast, athletic, aristocratic in appearance and bearing. Though happily married, Sherman's looks, friendly smile and full head of prematurely silver hair drew women to him like flies to honey.

"Uh-oh!" said Sherman, half-joking. "The word is out that something *always* happens when you get *that* feeling. I better recheck my gun. Maybe we'll get into a gun battle tonight. Wouldn't miss that for anything!"

"Okay, Tom. So, are we Three Zero Five, or Six?"

"Why not call in as Three Fifty-Six and see what Radio says?"

"I kind of like Three Sixty-Five better," Hitchcock quipped.

"We better call in as something before Breen gets upset."

Joking aside, Sherman believed in Hitchcock's gut feelings. He rechecked his revolver and spare ammunition pouches before leaving the station. He keyed the mike.

"Three Zero Five to Radio, 10-8 with Three Zero Six on board as a two-man unit covering Districts Five and Six."

"Received. Three Zero Five, now a two-man unit is back in service."

With Sherman driving, they returned to Eastgate.

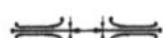

It was past midnight when Tyrone Hatch woke up in the ramshackle little rental house in lower Eastgate. He was alone except for the new girl he had locked up in a spare bedroom after shooting her up with her third dose of heroin. He would be leaving for a few hours, so he made her third dose stronger than usual.

For two days, Hatch had been snorting cocaine until he finally crashed. He left it to Mae to keep the other girl, Linda, busy turning tricks at his trailer in the trailer park next to the Hilltop while he slept.

Now Hatch was awake and aware that he was out of cocaine and heroin. He counted his cash before he called Marcellus, his contact in Seattle, to arrange a buy. He had twelve hundred. Not enough. *But when Mae brings the money Linda earned tonight, he thought, we should be able to buy enough to use and to sell. Provided, that is, that Linda doesn't try to hold back some of the money for herself.* He called Marcellus's number and hung up on the third ring. When he called back, Marcellus answered.

"Be at the same place as last time at two, with the cash, twenty-five bills," Marcellus told him. The call ended.

Moments later the kitchen phone rang. He stared at it, waiting. After the second ring, it stopped. Then it rang again. That was the signal that Mae was calling.

"How much?" he asked when he picked up the phone.

"Sixteen hundred, total. I got all of it. Linda wanted her share but I told her what she gets, if anything after last time, is up to you," Mae reported.

"Okay. Get here quick. We're goin' to meet Marcellus. Bring Linda with you for extra insurance, we'll make Marcellus think he can buy her. Hurry now. That Marcellus, he gets suspicious when anybody's late. I don't wanna be late."

After two days of snorting cocaine and not sleeping, paranoia dominated Tyrone's thought processes, even after he had slept. He was convinced someone was out to kill him. He was suspicious of everyone. It wasn't the police—he already knew they'd kill him if given even half a chance. Suddenly, in his drug-addled brain, he *knew* – Marcellus, his supplier, had turned snitch. Tonight, he'd get Marcellus's guard down, then kill him, get the dope, take his money, and leave his body for the cops to find. He checked his revolver, making sure it was loaded.

It was too dangerous to go to Seattle in the white Lincoln; the cops knew the car and they were looking for him. He would go in the dead girl's car, Janine's green Maverick. It had new, stolen plates on it. He loaded both barrels of his sawed-off shotgun and put two extra shells in his jacket pocket. He tucked his revolver in his waistband. Any cops who stopped him tonight would be dead meat. He checked on the new girl in the bedroom; still sleeping. *Good, tomorrow I'll put her to work,* he thought.

Mae arrived with Linda. Tyrone backed the Maverick out of the garage and parked the Cadillac inside. He handed Mae the key, and told her, "Marcellus's place. You drive --- Linda in front. I'll lay low in the back, out of sight. The pigs won't bother two white chicks and they don't know this car."

Mae checked her purse gun, a compact .380 caliber automatic, making sure its magazine was full with hollow-point bullets and a round was in the chamber. She drove through the sleeping neighborhood to the freeway overpass.

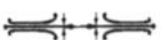

Hitchcock and Sherman sat in the Steak Out parking lot in view of the freeway overpass. They shared Army experiences to ease the tension they both felt. Hitchcock was talkative in the way of men who wait for the next battle to begin; it relieved tension.

"You were in the Rangers, a paratrooper," Hitchcock said, "I never could stand heights myself. Above seven or eight feet on a ladder I get butterflies, so I became a medic."

Sherman was only half-listening. The soldier in Sherman was telling him not to get too relaxed. Sergeant Breen alerting him about Tyrone Hatch wanting to kill an officer, and now Hitchcock's gut instinct acting up were enough to convince him that something was coming down. Talking about his Army days with a fellow ex-soldier both calmed him and kept him on alert at the same time.

"Heights never bothered me," Sherman said with a smile, "but the training to get into the 101st was the toughest thing I ever did. Eighty percent washout rate; but the effect on women of being in an elite unit made it worthwhile --"

"Hey Tom, look!" Hitchcock interrupted. "Is that a Ford Maverick crossing the overpass toward us?"

"Yeah! Definitely a Maverick. Can't tell the color from here in this light." Sherman said. He dropped the gear shift into drive. "I'll get close and you get the plate and run it."

"My informant told me tonight Hatch has a place in lower Eastgate, and we believe the girl who owned the Maverick got her heroin from Hatch. I took the stolen report. A witness saw a black male driving it from the victim's apartment," Hitchcock said.

"Hang on," Sherman said. He sped out of the Steak Out parking lot to the north end of the overpass and flashed his high beams to see the front plates on the approaching Maverick as he passed in the opposite direction. "Got it?"

"Yep" Hitchcock switched to Channel Two and keyed the mike. "Three Zero Five, Records, this is urgent: run a 10-28 [registration check] on Ocean Zebra Paul, Six Two One, Washington plate," he announced as Sherman hung a U-turn after they passed the Maverick.

"That's gotta be it. The Maverick is green, even has the damaged left fender. And those two broads look nervous," Sherman said.

Mae Driscoll panicked when in her rear-view mirror she saw the Bellevue black-and-white flip a U-turn. In her confusion, she missed the on-ramp to the westbound freeway. She stopped at the red signal facing the T-intersection, not knowing what to do next, her pulse racing as the patrol car came up behind her.

"Tyrone, we got trouble!" Mae shouted to Hatch, on the rear floor.

"Talk to me! What's goin' on? I can tell you didn't make that turn onto the freeway!" Hatch shouted.

Mae's heart was racing. "Bellevue PD behind us right now! Two pigs in the car!"

"Damn! Get us outta here! Drive! Drive!" Hatch shouted, heart pounding, sweating profusely, laying on the rear floor, both hands clutching his shotgun.

Mae froze with fear. She sat through a green signal with the police car right behind her. The red overhead light of the police car behind her came on. As the signal turned to red again, she suddenly turned left against the red light into the intersection, heading toward the Steak Out.

Hitchcock and Sherman listened as Records came back with the report: "Three Zero Five, Ocean Zebra Paul Six Two One are stolen plates belonging on a white 1966 Chevy Malibu, registered owner in Seattle."

Sherman activated the siren as he followed the Ford Maverick.

Hitchcock felt his heart rate increase. "That's it, the Maverick belonging to Janine Collins," he said.

They followed the Maverick as it turned left onto 148th Avenue for a block, then right onto the frontage road, at speeds below the speed limit. Instead of pulling over, it continued westbound on the two-lane frontage road, weaving erratically, increasing speed.

"Looks like the women are fighting! They just missed the last on-ramp if they're trying to get to Seattle," Sherman said, his heart racing now.

Hitchcock switched back to Channel One. "Three Zero Five, Radio, request assistance stopping a suspected stolen vehicle, a green Ford Maverick with dented fender, bearing stolen Washington plates Ocean Zebra Paul Six Two One. It's headed westbound onto the north frontage road passing Lakeside Sand and Gravel, two white female subjects aboard."

Sergeant Breen came on the air. "Four Twenty is close by and en route to assist Three Zero Five, Radio."

Dispatch came on the air. "10-4. All units, emergency traffic only."

The Maverick and Sherman's patrol car were the only cars on the frontage road when Sherman sounded the siren again. At thirty miles per hour the Maverick swerved over the centerline again below a crest in the hill, then over-corrected to the right, crashing into a telephone pole with its right front fender.

Sherman spotlighted the car's rear window. The heads of two occupants in the front seat could be seen; neither was moving. Sherman thought the occupants had to be injured or unconscious from the crash. Hitchcock keyed the radio mike:

> "Three Zero Five, Radio, suspect vehicle just crashed into a telephone pole on the frontage road in front of the Lakeside Sand and Gravel pit at a speed of about thirty. The occupants in the front seat are visible but aren't moving. We'll be checking for injuries. Get an ambulance on the way."

Shining flashlights into the rear window, they walked up to the wrecked vehicle from the rear, Hitchcock on the right, Sherman on the left. As they passed the tail-lights of the Maverick, a shotgun blast blew the rear window out, splattering the chests of both officers with glass fragments. Hitchcock and Sherman drew their revolvers. Hitchcock opened fire first at a black male adult on the rear floor who was aiming a double-barrel shotgun at them. Sherman began firing at a burst of light and a gunshot that came from the front seat of the Maverick as Hitchcock continued shooting.

In the ferocious exchange of gunfire at point--blank range, both officers descended into survival mode, to the lowest level of their training. Reality narrowed to a tunnel as they returned fire without thought, heart rates skyrocketing, seeing in slow motion the man with the shotgun in the back seat, who was about to shoot again, trying to kill him before he could fire the other barrel.

Hitchcock and Sherman were suddenly clicking triggers on empty guns. Neither could remember how many rounds they had fired, nor did they know if the man with the shotgun had fired again before he slipped from view. They were unaware that Sergeant Breen had arrived as it happened and had called in the shooting.

Hitchcock was certain the man in the back was dead, but there were two people in the front seat who could be armed. Remembering the details of the four officers killed in the Newhall incident in California earlier in the year, he quickly walked backwards in a half-crouch, checking to stay abreast of Sherman, opening the cylinder of his revolver, shucking empty shell cases that clattered on the asphalt pavement, opening the cruiser passenger door to use as a shield as he unsnapped one of his two spare ammo pouches. Only three of the six rounds in the first pouch fell out.

With fingers stiff with fear he slipped the live rounds into the chambers and loaded three more from the second pouch. He closed the cylinder and remained kneeling behind the door, gun aimed at the Maverick.

Hitchcock checked himself over. "I'm not hurt, Tom! I see movement in the front seat, right side!"

Sherman had retreated to his vehicle for cover alongside Hitchcock. He had reloaded already. Now he grabbed his radio mike. "Shots fired, Radio! Officers not hurt. One suspect believed dead!"

Sergeant Breen was positioned behind Hitchcock and Sherman. He got on the radio again. "Four-Twenty is at the scene, Radio.

Confirming shots fired, officers not hurt, one suspect in the other car believed dead. Get the on-call detective supervisor to send two detectives, get an ETA from the ambulance, get a second ambulance on the way!"

Sherman saw movement in the Maverick, followed by a woman's wailing. "Help me! Oh God, somebody help me!"

The woman behind the wheel was slumped onto the steering wheel, motionless; the passenger was writhing in her seat, groaning and pleading "Help! Don't ... don't let her shoot me again."

Sergeant Breen aimed his vehicle spotlight through the blown out right rear window of the Maverick, illuminating the interior. He could see the heads of two occupants on the front seat. He positioned Hitchcock and Sherman on either side of the rear to cover him as he approached on the right side and checked the interior, gun in one hand, flashlight in the other.

Breen had never seen or imagined anything like this in his eleven years on the job, nor in his peacetime stint in the Army. The man on the back floor lay motionless. There were multiple gunshot wounds to the head, his mouth was gaping open, his face was unrecognizable; a short-barrel shotgun was lying on his lap. A slender young woman with brown hair in the front passenger seat was conscious and moaning, her hands palms-up in her lap in a gesture of surrender. Breen saw a stocky young woman with bleached hair in the driver seat was stone still, lips parted, eyes staring. Breen leaned across the passenger, and took the driver's wrist to feel her pulse. She, too, was dead.

The passenger had lost much blood and was going into shock. She mumbled something about getting another fix. Sergeant Breen waved the arriving ambulance crew in, indicating it was safe for them to approach. He saw that she was bleeding from the left side of her abdomen. She was awake but losing consciousness. She looked up at Sergeant Breen. Death was in her eyes.

"What's your name, Miss?" Breen asked.

"Linda. They've got another girl in their house. They've been keeping her prisoner since they kidnapped her. She's hooked now. You've *got* to help her, but please don't tell Mae or Tyrone I told you. They'll kill me."

To Breen's own surprise, a sense of bravado and gallows humor came out. "Naw," he said matter-of-factly. "They won't be bothering anybody any-more, Miss. I promise you that. They're both dead. Now who is this girl and where is she?"

Linda looked from Breen to Hitchcock and back again. "They're dead? Both dead? How? I can't believe it!"

"Believe it. They made the mistake of tangling with my boys. Now tell me who is the man in the back and where is the girl being held?"

Linda was fading. "Tyrone--Tyrone Hatch," she replied. "His house is a small, brown house a block up from the gas station. She's locked in a back bedroom; a nice kid. You've *got* to check on her."

"We'll find her right away. What's her name?" Breen asked.

Linda was becoming slower to answer. Her eyes were beginning to close. "Claudia ----- something. She's---missing ----from---- Everett," she slurred as she slipped into unconsciousness.

"I can go, Sarge," Hitchcock offered.

"Nope. You and Sherman were just involved in a shooting; you'll both stay until detectives get here."

Sergeant Breen keyed his radio. "Four-Twenty to Three Zero Seven?"

Otis answered. "Three Zero Seven."

"Respond immediately to the scene here on the frontage road for an urgent detail. Code Two."

"10-4, Three Zero Seven, en route," Otis replied.

The first news reporter arrived, then another, then another. It amused Breen that reporters had arrived before the detectives did. He warned the reporters to stay back, and began cordoning off the scene with barrier tape. Sherman helped him, then Hitchcock. Afterward, Breen looked into the blood-soaked front seat again with his flashlight. The back of the driver's clothing was drenched in blood. He saw a glint of metal on the middle of the front seat. Looking closely, he saw two shell casings. *Were these fired tonight? So where's the gun?*

Tom Sherman's adrenalin rush began to subside as he helped secure the scene. He waited for the detectives to arrive. A familiar feeling of elation came over him. Once again, he had survived deadly combat, and once again he felt intensely alive. Instinctively his hand felt for his gun to re-snap the holster strap. His gun was there but the strap wouldn't close. He looked down. It was broken. He showed it to Hitchcock.

"See this, Roger?" Sherman said, grinning. "I drew my gun right through the leather. Next time we work together and you get one of your gut feelings that something's gonna happen, I got dibs on the shotgun!"

Hitchcock grinned but said nothing. He too had that familiar "Thank God it wasn't me" feeling of relief and gratitude to be alive. His senses were always sharpest after a brush with Death. He felt little granules on the pocket seams of his uniform shirt. They were tiny lead pellets.

"Hey Tom," Hitchcock said with a grin, "lucky for us Hatch was using birdshot. We'd be hurt, or dead for sure if he had double-ought buck in his shotgun."

Sherman smiled and nodded as if he had been told his shoelaces were loose. That was Tom Sherman.

Hitchcock checked the condition of his own holster. He too had drawn his gun right through the leather retention strap, breaking it in the middle. A flashing red light in the distance caught his eye. It was Joel Otis, up the frontage road, approaching the scene in his patrol car, Code Two…

To be continued.

The saga continues in Book Three …

Valley Of Long Shadows

Order more books at
Amazon Books.com, or
www.bluesuitchronicles.com
Contact the Author at
John@bluesuitchronicles.com
Bluesuit Chronicles on Facebook
Google: John Hansen Historical Crime Fiction Novels

Books by John Hansen

Song of the Waterwheel

The Bluesuit Chronicles Series:
The War Comes Home
The New Darkness
Valley of Long Shadows
Day Shift
Unfinished Business

Published and Award-Winning Essays
Losing Kristene
Riding the Superstitions
The Case of the Old Colt
Charlie's Story
The Mystery of Three

Copies of other books in The Bluesuit Chronicles series can be purchased through Amazon.com. Individual books can be previewed and purchased directly from our website at www.bluesuitchronicles.com.

Made in the USA
San Bernardino, CA
24 January 2018